CROSSFIRE

**NEW
ISLAND**

CROSSFIRE

The Battle of the Four Courts, 1916

PAUL O'BRIEN

1916 IN FOCUS

CROSSFIRE
First published 2012
by New Island
2 Brookside
Dundrum Road
Dublin 14
www.newisland.ie

P/B   ISBN 978-1- 84840-129-7
ePub   ISBN 978-1- 84840-144-0
emobi   ISBN 978-1- 84840-145-7

British Library Cataloguing Data. A CIP catalogue record for this book is
available from the British Library.

Typeset by Mariel Deegan
Cover design by Justin Deegan
Printed by Bell & Bain Ltd., Glasgow

New Island received financial assistance from
The Arts Council (An Comhairle Ealaíon), Dublin, Ireland

10 9 8 7 6 5 4 3 2 1

*'Better to write for yourself and have no public
than to write for the public and have no self.'*
Cyril Conway

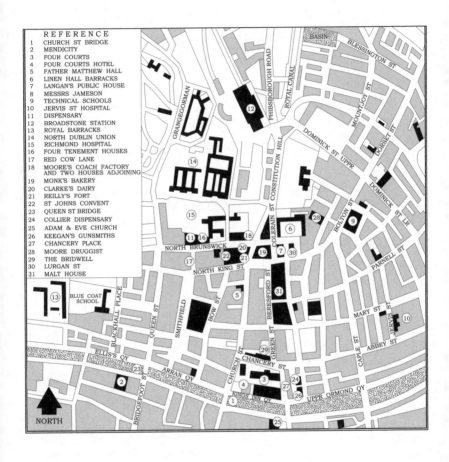

REFERENCE
1   CHURCH ST BRIDGE
2   MENDICITY
3   FOUR COURTS
4   FOUR COURTS HOTEL
5   FATHER MATTHEW HALL
6   LINEN HALL BARRACKS
7   LANGAN'S PUBLIC HOUSE
8   MESSRS JAMESON
9   TECHNICAL SCHOOLS
10 JERVIS ST HOSPITAL
11 DISPENSARY
12 BROADSTONE STATION
13 ROYAL BARRACKS
14 NORTH DUBLIN UNION
15 RICHMOND HOSPITAL
16 FOUR TENEMENT HOUSES
17 RED COW LANE
18 MOORE'S COACH FACTORY
    AND TWO HOUSES ADJOINING
19 MONK'S BAKERY
20 CLARKE'S DAIRY
21 REILLY'S FORT
22 ST JOHNS CONVENT
23 QUEEN ST BRIDGE
24 COLLIER DISPENSARY
25 ADAM & EVE CHURCH
26 KEEGAN'S GUNSMITHS
27 CHANCERY PLACE
28 MOORE DRUGGIST
29 THE BRIDWELL
30 LURGAN ST
31 MALT HOUSE

Contents

Acknowledgements

In writing on the military aspects of the 1916 Rising, I count myself extremely fortunate to have been in contact with so many extraordinary and generous people.

I would like to thank Patrick Holohan and the Holohan family, and also Chris Shouldice and his family for the information they provided on their relatives. This book could not have been written without their assistance, and I am delighted to acknowledge them here.

I would like also to express my gratitude to the hard-working staff of the following archives, libraries, museums and other institutions who have gone out of their way to make my job as easy and as enjoyable as possible: the National Archives, Dublin, Military Archives at Cathal Brugha Barracks, Dublin, Kilmainham Gaol Archives, the museum of The Staffordshire Regiment, The Queen's Royal Lancers Museum, The National Library, Ballymun Library and the Library of the Office of Public Works.

I would like to thank Dr Mary Montaut and John McGuiggan, who took the time to read the initial drafts of the book, for their help and constructive criticism, which is greatly appreciated.

Throughout the writing of this book, I have had the remarkable assistance of two very fine researchers: Elizabeth Gillis and

Sue Sutton. Their contribution to this book has been of inestimable value and I profoundly thank them.

Many thanks also to Tony Rowe, Conor and Liam Dodd for information on the Royal Dublin Fusiliers.

For mapping the field of battle, special words of thanks are due to Gerry Woods.

I would like to thank the following for their assistance, insight, encouragement and advice: Henry Fairbrother, Ernie Waters, Ray Bateson, Las Fallon, Ronnie Daly, Wayne Fitzgerald, James Langton, Gretta Halpin and Mick O'Farrell.

Grateful thanks are due to Charlie Carroll, Charlie Thomas and Colm Naughton for the early-morning discussions on the topography of Dublin city.

I would like to thank Eoin Purcell and the staff of New Island Books for their crucial role in bringing this story to the public.

For their humour and companionship, thanks to Michael Cahill, Darren O'Brien and Tommy Galvin.

My deepest gratitude goes to my parents Tommy and Rita, and to my wife Marian O'Brien, whose continuous support and encouragement is, as always, greatly appreciated.

This book has been written using the available historical records both in England and Ireland. There are many, many people who helped with my research, and in naming some of them I can only apologise to those whom I may have inadvertently left out. I would like to invite them to make me aware of any omissions or relevant information that may be included in any future updated edition.

Paul O'Brien
Dublin, February 2012
paulobrienauthor.ie

A Note on the 1916 in Focus Series

As the centenary of the 1916 Rising approaches dozens of books will be published on the events and people involved. There is a danger in this increased output, much of it focused on the broad sweep of the Rising, that the macro will swamp the micro, that small pictures of the history that illuminate and describe particular aspects of the Rising will be lost.

This series of short, accessible and informative books (and ebooks) on very specific aspects of the Rising or individual events is an attempt to ensure that does not happen.

Future volumes in the series will look at the aftermath of the Rising, at the experience of Volunteer prisoners after the Rising and at the ideology that underpinned those involved in the rising. It won't simply focus on the Irish side of the event either.

In short the series will concentrate on the micro-histories of the Rising and in doing so make the macro picture that bit more textured, detailed and true to life.

Eoin Purcell
Series Commissioning Editor

Introduction

Dublin's Four Courts, located on Inns Quay, is one of the most recognisable buildings in Ireland. Designed and built by James Gandon in 1785, this landmark edifice opened its doors in November 1796. Since then the building has been the centre of the administration of justice in Ireland. On entering through the imposing front door, a large, round hall leads to the four courts of Chancery, Exchequer, King's Bench and Common Pleas, now more commonly known as courts one, two, three and four. The round hall of the Four Courts, with its Corinthian columns and ornate dome, dominates the skyline of Dublin city. The buildings contained a records office and archive that held papers dating back to the eleventh century. The complex itself was a central point during the 1916 Rising. Later it was almost destroyed in 1922 during the Irish Civil War. In 1932 the building was restored but the interior was planned to a different style.

Outside its railings and high walls, running adjacent to the Courts complex, is Church Street, stretching from Arran Quay up to Constitution Hill. Its name derives from the church dedicated to St Michan the martyr. At numbers 131-137 is the Father Matthew Temperance Hall and beside it, at number 138, stands the Franciscan Capuchin Friary built in 1881. A little further on, Church Street intersects with North King Street. Stretching from Stoneybatter through Smithfield to Bolton Street, this sixteenth century street formed part of an area that became so populated, that a new and separate parish was created in 1697. Once an affluent area of Dublin, by 1916 it had become an area known for poverty, with many tenements and huckster shops.

Today, it is hard to imagine that this busy and impressive complex and the adjacent thoroughfare were witness to one of the greatest battles of the 1916 Rising. It was at the Four Courts and in the surrounding area that a small force of Irish Volunteers held out against overwhelming odds for one week in April 1916. Like every strategic battle, it included a number of smaller actions during that week that were bitterly contested. This urban battlefield would be witness to some of the most advanced tactical manoeuvres of the time and also some of the most horrific atrocities seen that Easter week. In order to guide the reader through the complex battlefield of the Four Courts I have created a map designed to provide a unique visual approach to the area. Buildings and locations followed by (x) are included in the map with x indicating the corresponding number on the chart. On the first occasion the building appears in a section it will be referenced to facilitate readers.

On Easter Monday, 24 April 1916, Patrick Pearse, Commander-in-Chief of the Irish Volunteers, issued a proclamation declaring an independent Irish Republic. In order to defend this newly declared republic, 1,500 men, women and teenage boys and girls of the Volunteer movement occupied a number of strategic buildings within Dublin city. By the end of Easter week this small force would be in direct conflict with over 20,000 British troops.

Members of the 1st Battalion of the Irish Volunteers under the leadership of Commandant Edward Daly occupied the Four Courts and the surrounding area of Church Street and North King Street. During the week that followed, some of the toughest fighting seen in Dublin city took place within this area. Elements of the 1st Battalion were the last Volunteer units to surrender during the 1916 Rising after receiving orders issued directly by Patrick Pearse.

The battle that erupted in and around the Four Courts was a haphazard and unruly confrontation over a large and highly obstructive battleground. The complexity of the battle posed tactical problems for the defenders as well as those attacking them.

In previous campaigns the British Army relied on sheer weight of men and materials in order to turn the tide of battle. During the Easter Rising of 1916 the British military discovered that it was no longer possible, as had been common practice, to overwhelm the enemy by launching larger numbers of men at a vital point in the confrontation.

This battle poses a number of questions to the student of military history. Firstly in relation to the overall strategy employed by the British commander, Brigadier General W.H.M. Lowe, and whether the area could have been cordoned off, avoiding the ensuing confrontation and loss of life. On the ground the British commander of the North Staffordshire regiment, Lieutenant-Colonel Henry Taylor, utilised techniques that would have been considered unorthodox at the time, in order to gain a foothold in the area. Was he correct to do so?

On the Irish side, the countermanding order issued by Eoin MacNeill must once again be questioned, as it left Daly's Battalion dangerously under strength. Examining the defensive urban warfare conducted by Daly is instructive for modern armies, even now. These same methods and techniques are still used throughout the world, and form the basis of defending and attacking in a built-up area.

Commandant Daly's Irish Volunteers and Lieutenant-Colonel Taylor and the North Staffordshire regiment were detailed to undertake some of the most demanding and important tasks of any of the other battalions that Easter week. Under appalling conditions, both sides fought for a cause that they believed was just.

The innocent civilians killed in this area during the 1916 Rising remain faceless, assigned to a forgotten grave in a lonely graveyard. It is difficult to find out exactly what happens in combat. Regimental histories and war diaries can gloss over unsavoury details, and the usual correlation of historical records in relation to the Rising is not possible as few records exist to be compared.

Much of what is written within these pages is taken from witness statements and interviews with those who survived that week. Individual memories of the Rising are often at odds with history books, autobiographies and official regimental diaries. For many reasons the truth is often altered or omitted from published accounts.

What follows is the story of 1916 and the battle for the Four Courts and North King Street.

Chapter 1

Easter Monday 24 April 1916: Morning

At 11.00 hours on the morning of Easter Monday, 24 April 1916, members of the 1st Battalion of the Irish Volunteers mobilised at the Colmcille Hall, Blackhall Place, Dublin. As the Volunteers entered the hall they noticed the company officers at the head of the room in conversation with the Battalion's commander, Commandant Edward (Ned) Daly.

Born into a prominent republican family in County Limerick in 1891, Daly had joined the Irish Volunteers on their foundation in November 1913 and rose rapidly through the ranks. At twenty-five years of age he was the youngest man to hold the rank of commandant in the organisation. Daly was the younger brother of Kathleen Clarke, the wife of Tom Clarke, a noted republican and a signatory of the Irish Proclamation. Daly's command of the 1st Battalion and his military efficiency impressed his superiors. His serious expression and dark, sad eyes masked his skill as a military tactician and strategist.

Assisting Daly was Vice-Commandant Piaras Béaslaí. Born in Liverpool in 1881, Béaslaí moved to Dublin in 1904. There he joined the Gaelic League and became an ardent promoter of the Irish language. He founded the Society of Gaelic Writers and the newspaper *An Fáinne*. A member of the Irish Republican Brotherhood (IRB), he joined the Volunteer movement in 1914.

Daly took to the podium and ordered the Volunteers to fall in. He addressed them, stating that a provisional government had been formed and that an Irish Republic would be declared at noon. In the course of his address he emphasised the fact that the men would be required to defend that republic with their lives, but if there was any man present who felt he could not comply with this order he could withdraw and nothing the worse would be thought of him. Only two men withdrew while the others cheered loudly. The time was 11.45 hours.[1]

The Battalion was weakened due to an order that Eoin Mac Neill, Chief of Staff of the Volunteers, issued on the Easter Saturday rescinding the orders for manoeuvres on Easter Sunday. MacNeill, a member of the supreme council of the IRB, withdrew his support for the Rising having heard that Roger Casement had been arrested and that the *Aud*, a ship laden with arms and ammunition, had been intercepted by the Royal Navy. Not only was the rescinding order published in the national press, but it was also distributed by courier throughout the rest of the country. The Rising, originally planned for Easter Sunday, was postponed, but the military council of the IRB decided to go ahead and ordered a mobilisation for Easter Monday. Only 130 Volunteers, Fianna Éireann and Cumann na mBan had turned out from a 1st Battalion force that normally numbered 400. However, their ranks would increase in the coming days as the news of the Rising spread. As the Volunteers left the hall, they were given extra rounds of ammunition. They formed into ranks outside and began marching towards their designated battalion area, The Four Courts [3].

The 1st Battalion's principal objective was to occupy and hold the law courts on Inns Quay and the adjacent streets on the north side of the River Liffey. The Battalion was to occupy a line that ran from the Four Courts on the north bank of the Liffey to Cabra, where it was to link up with the 5th Battalion under the command of Commandant Thomas Ashe. This strategic location controlled the main approach routes from the west of Dublin to the centre of the city. The area was almost a mile to the west of the General Post Office where the new provisional government had established their General Headquarters (GHQ).

Daly set up Battalion staff headquarters in the Convent of St John [22] between North King Street and North Brunswick Street. Here he was welcomed with enthusiasm from the patriotic French Sisters of Charity and Father Albert OSF and Father Augustine OSF.

Adjutant Eamon Duggan and quartermaster Eamon Morkan began distributing arms and ammunition that had been deposited in safe houses in the area in the weeks leading to Easter Monday. Daly's force was significantly depleted, and though he had six companies of Volunteers they consisted in some cases of only five men. It was vital that Volunteer forces be deployed rapidly to ensure they caught the British forces by surprise. Béaslaí directed his forces with urgency, as he knew it would be only a matter of time before the British crown forces would retaliate.

'A' Company, commanded by Captain Denis O'Callaghan, was ordered to occupy the Broadstone Railway Station [12] (the terminus of the Midland Great Western Railway). However, acting on his own initiative he felt that his small unit was insufficient to undertake such a task and instead detailed his men to occupy tenement houses on North King Street. A nearby builder's yard provided the Volunteers with barrels, bags of sand, planks, scaffolding poles and vehicles that were used to block the street. Buildings were pierced periodically with loopholes. These holes were then disguised and camouflaged to avoid detection by the enemy. Their purpose was for observation and sniping. Doors were barricaded and windows were sandbagged and prepared for defence. Monk's Bakery [19] was occupied and the staff was permitted to continue working as the Volunteers began fortifying the post with sacks of flour and loop-holing the walls for firing positions. At the narrowest part of Church Street, Commandant Daly ordered 12 men to occupy Clarke's Dairy [20]. This three-storey building had a commanding view of Constitution Hill and the approach from the Broadstone Railway Station. The walls were loop-holed and the Volunteers took up firing positions that enabled them to provide mutual support to other posts.

'B' Company, under Captain James Sullivan, erected barricades on the northern flank at the North Circular Road and the Cabra Road while engineer Captain Frank Daly proceeded to destroy some of the railway infrastructure in the area. This position was strategically important as it provided a line of retreat for the Battalion to North County Dublin.

'C' Company, under the command of Captain Frank Fahy and Lieutenant Joseph McGuinness, occupied the Four Courts [3]. Sittings in the court had been suspended for the Easter holiday. Lieutenant Thomas Allen, revolver in hand, relieved a solitary policeman of his keys to the building, and the Volunteers gained entry to the courts complex through Chancery Place [27]. The caretaker who was found in the basement was permitted to leave. Telephone lines were cut, and the Volunteers set about fortifying their position. The gates to the complex were secured, windows were smashed and barricaded with tables and chairs. Leather-bound ledgers, law books and legal documents also found their way into the defence structures. Sandbags were filled and placed in position. Snipers took up position on the roof, and a tricolour was unfurled.

The windows of the Chancellor's office were barricaded by Charles Bevan and three others. Large, leather-bound books were taken from the library and placed on the window-sills. Beds from the nearby Four Courts Hotel [4] were commandeered and carried to the Chancellor's office as the Volunteers established a makeshift First Aid post.

'F' Company, under Captain Fionan Lynch, began to dig in on the greater part of Church Street. Three barricades were constructed along this length of roadway. The first was located at the junction of the quays and Church Street facing Church Street Bridge [1]. This lower obstruction was manned by a section of men under Peadar Clancy. Halfway up Church Street, outside the church, a brick bulwark was constructed spanning the roadway. Bedsteads were linked across the road and cobblestones were prised up to make improvised walls. Building materials from a building site opposite the church provided the materials required to construct barricades in the small lanes and side-streets off Church Street. Glass and broken bottles were strewn in front of some of the barricades to impede an attack by cavalry. At the upper end of the street, at the junction of Church Street and North King Street, a barricade spanning the roadway was erected.

Members of the Cumann na mBan, the female section of the Volunteers, were divided into two groups. The first section donned Red Cross armbands and established a hospital in the Father Matthew Hall [5] on Church Street and within the Four Courts. Staff officer Martin Conlon oversaw the establishment of these posts. A kitchen was also set up to provide food to the Volunteers. While most of the Volunteers carried twenty-four hours of rations, food was commandeered from local shops and stockpiled in the hall. The second Cumann na mBan unit were required to travel from post to post issuing food, ammunition and despatches. They also scouted the streets in order to locate any troop movements. In the coming days they were to play a vital role in keeping the communication lines open.

'G' Company was captained by Nicholas Laffan, whose force occupied buildings on North King Street and Brunswick Street. A barricade was erected at the eastern end of Brunswick Street where it reached Upper Church Street. Milk floats and lorries were dragged from Moore's [18] the coachbuilders and placed across the road diagonally, linking Moore's coach factory to North Brunswick Street. This barricade consisted of a cab that served as a control point for exit and entrance to Brunswick Street and Church Street. It was placed so that one had to pass through the doors of the cab in order to get into Brunswick Street. Volunteers took up firing positions in Moore's and two tenement houses adjoining the works. Further down North Brunswick Street, Lieutenant Liam O'Carroll drew his revolver and blew the lock off the gate of Cullen's Builders' yard. The men hauled out four-wheeled lorries, timber and heavy building material in order to erect a barricade across the street, one on each side of Red Cow Lane [17], near Daly's Headquarters. Four men were left on guard duty at the barricades while others began evacuating four tenement houses [16]. When the houses were cleared, the walls were knocked through, linking each building and providing the men with adequate cover. A dispensary [11] was also occupied and barricaded. Waste material was used to fill bags that were then placed in the windows. The men were withdrawn from the street and took up positions at the windows covering the barricades. An obstruction was erected across Bow Lane with materials requisitioned from Jameson's Distillery [8].[2]

Traversing Daly's command was North King Street. At the upper end of the street a section under Tom Sheeran occupied Langan's Public House [7] at the corner of North King Street and Coleraine Street. A barricade was constructed outside the building and the men took up positions at the windows covering the barricade. This post would cover any attack made from the Bolton Street direction.

The greatest concentration of posts was located at the other end of the street, where North King Street intersects with Church Street. At this intersection three barricades blocked the junction, and a public house (later to be known as 'Reilly's Fort' [21]) at the corner of North King Street and Church Street was occupied by a group of Volunteers commanded by Lieutenant Jack Shouldice. This strategic position connected Daly's command north and south of the battalion area. On entering the building the small garrison began to reinforce the window positions with sacks of meal and flour taken from the Blanchardstown Mill shop. The front door was barricaded and the men took up firing positions throughout the Public House.

Frank Shouldice, the younger brother of Jack, occupied the Jameson Malt House Tower [31] on Beresford Street. This post overlooked North King Street and gave a commanding view of the area.

Locals reluctantly left their houses with what few possessions they could carry and obtained shelter in places outside the battalion's area. Many were permitted to bring their belongings to the North Dublin Union [14] or to the Technical Schools [9] in Bolton Street. A stream of refugees made their way out of the area but many others chose to stay.

The only company not present in the area was 'D' company. Captain Séan Heuston and 'D' Company of the 1st Battalion assembled at Mountjoy Square and marched to Liberty Hall. His unit consisted of 12 young men of the Fianna Éireann movement. Commandant James Connolly of the Irish Citizen Army deployed Heuston's unit to occupy the Mendicity Institute [2] as an outpost on the south side of the River Liffey at Ushers Quay, about half a mile to the west of the Four Courts. Heuston's section were ordered to control the route between the Royal Barracks [13] (now the National Museum, Collins Barracks) and the Four Courts in order to give Daly's garrison time to establish its defences. It was envisaged that this would only take a few hours and that Heuston could then withdraw from the post.

The Mendicity Institute, located on Ushers Island along the River Liffey, was a large, stone building that catered for many of Dublin's homeless. When the young Volunteers arrived they began occupying the rooms at the front of the building. The staff and the unfortunate down-and-outs were hustled at gunpoint through the basement dining hall, across the courtyard and out into the street. The large, wooden gates were closed and the

Volunteers immediately began barricading the windows on the top floor of the building. Furniture was manhandled into windows, glass was smashed out of the frames and curtains were ripped down and stuffed in between the sashes and the furniture to act as sandbags. To reduce the chance of wounds from flying fragments, glass ornaments, cases and vases were smashed. In case of fire, buckets of water were placed at strategic points throughout the building. The Volunteers had turned the building into a compact strong-point. Lieutenant Willie Murnane, Dick Balfe, Liam Staines and Eddie Roache took up position at the windows. Volunteer Patrick Stephenson, looking out the top window of the building, wrote:

...I looked through the window and there, with his elbows resting on the stone plinth of the front wall, was a tall D.M.P.[3] man. Under the dark blue helmet, with its silver facing, there was a big, soft face with big eyes, like those of an oxen. His big mouth was wide open with astonishment. After a minute he raised his voice and shouted in a broad country accent, 'eh, you fellows are going too far with this playing at soldiers. Don't you know you can be arrested for what yez are doing?' The unconscious remark struck me as very funny and I burst out laughing. A voice from some part of the building shouted, 'Be off to hell out of that, if you don't want a bullet in your thick skull!' but without effect. He stood where he was seemingly incapable of movement. Again the same voice shouted. 'You big ejit, why don't you take yourself off while you are alive? Don't you know the republic has been proclaimed and your bloody day is done?' and punctuated his remarks by firing off a round.

The sound of the revolver shot galvanised the Peeler into action and he shot off down the quays so quickly that his helmet fell off his head.[4]

Heuston ordered his men to be vigilant and said, 'When the troops move out of the barracks wait until they are right opposite to you before opening fire. A blast on my whistle will be the signal to fire.'[5]

Chapter 2

Easter Monday 24 April 1916: First Blood

At 12.00 hours another unit of the 1st Battalion were moving into position. Fianna Éireann Volunteers Patrick and Garry Holohan were members of a 30-strong 1st Battalion Special Forces unit led by Paddy Daly. Their task was to signal the beginning of the Rising by an explosion at the Magazine Fort located in the Phoenix Park. This complex held the British military's reserve of explosives, ammunition and ordnance.

Located on Thomas's Hill in the Phoenix Park, the Magazine Fort overhangs the Chapelizod Road. Its defences consisted of 8 feet thick walls topped with granite blocks. Each corner of the fort had a sentry tower with a pintle mounting for a Vickers machine gun. A steep ditch with only one entry/exit point that was accessible by a drawbridge surrounded the compound. British soldiers patrolled the battlements and sentries guarded the gate.

Six months previously Daly had been employed by Shortall's Building Contractors. This company was engaged in carrying out works on the complex and Daly had gained detailed knowledge of the layout of the fort and the garrison's roster. In order to move close to the fort without alarming the guard, the Volunteers began a football match near the complex. The time was 12.17 hours. The ball was soon kicked over the perimeter wall. The Volunteers approached the gate and asked the sentry 'Would you mind returning the ball, please?' As he turned to retrieve the ball the gate was rushed and the sentry was overpowered. Dashing through the entrance, the other Volunteers quickly overpowered and disarmed the ten soldiers in the guardroom. Mrs Isabel Playfair, the wife of the Fort's commander (on active service in France), and her three children were also held captive.

Volunteers Garry Holohan and Barney Mellowes were detailed to take care of the sentry on the parapet. Holohan made his way past the guardroom and through a long passageway, emerging in a bright quadrangle with a raised platform 4 feet high, which ran around the walls. In the corners there were short, stone staircases. A British soldier stood with his back to the Volunteer. Holohan drew his .22 automatic pistol and ordered the soldier to surrender. The soldier turned around and attempted to aim his rifle but was obstructed by a building that blocked his target. Unable to fire, the soldier lowered his weapon and attempted to affix his bayonet in order to challenge Holohan. Holohan rushed forward and fired twice at the soldier, hitting him in the thigh.[1] The soldier dropped his weapon and collapsed on the ground writhing in agony. Mellowes arrived and attempted to lift the soldier to his feet but the man collapsed. Holohan contacted the Volunteers holding the prisoners and ordered that the British soldiers carry the wounded man to the guardroom.

The prisoners were informed that the magazine was to be destroyed and that they had 6 minutes to evacuate the complex. The group was warned that once outside they were not to attempt to raise an alarm.

Having secured the compound, the Volunteers set about their mission to destroy the fort. They sought the key to the high explosives store that hung on a board in the office. To their dismay they discovered that the officer in charge of the fort had accidentally placed the key to the stores in his pocket and had gone to the Fairyhouse races. Undaunted, Patrick Holohan assisted by Edward Martin and the demolition squad gathered any small ordnance they could locate to act as an incendiary. They began entering the other storerooms, setting their fuses, locking the doors and throwing the keys back into the stores. The insurgents had been trained in the use of explosives and they placed their five bags of gelignite against the wall of the main magazine in the hope that the explosion would blow through the wall and ignite the main stores. Garry Holohan set the fuses and quickly withdrew.

All the arms and ammunition in the small-arms store were collected and taken outside. A hackney car was commandeered and Daly ordered the weapons to be loaded into the well of the vehicle. Volunteers Daly, Martin and Mellows along with Tim Roche, Séan O'Briain, Paddy Holohan and Jack Murphy all climbed aboard the hackney while the others headed back towards their designated battalion areas on foot and on bicycles.

Garry Holohan, acting as a scout, accompanied the hackney on his bicycle. Daly shouted to Holohan that Mrs

Playfair's 14-year-old son, Gerald, was running ahead of them trying to raise the alarm. The boy ran out the park gate and crossed the Chapelizod Road and spoke briefly to a policeman. He then ran on towards Islandbridge and the nearby barracks. Garry Holohan cycled frantically in order to intercept the boy before he raised the alarm. The boy reached the corner of Islandbridge Road and made for a large row of houses that included the residence of the barrack commander. Without stopping, the boy frantically glanced around and saw the Volunteer giving chase on the bicycle. He quickened his pace and fled through the garden gate and ran up the pathway knocking furiously on the front door. Holohan pulled up outside the house, dropping the bicycle to the ground. As he reached the bottom of the path, Playfair looked back at Holohan from the doorway. As the door opened, Holohan opened fire with his automatic pistol hitting the boy three times. Mortally wounded, Gerald slumped in the doorway. As Holohan remounted his bicycle he heard a muffled explosion in the distance as the fuses in the fort expired. They had failed to ignite the main explosives store, signalling the beginning of the Rising. The Volunteers made their way back to the Four Courts, where they distributed the captured arms and ammunition and then took up position with their designated companies. The Irish Volunteers had drawn first blood.

Chapter 3

Easter Monday 24 April 1916: Afternoon

Shortly after 12.00 hours, a detachment of 50 Lancers of the 6th Reserve Cavalry regiment (5th & 12th Lancers) under the command of Second Lieutenant Godfrey Jackson Hunter rode along the North Quays from the direction of the North Wall. The contingent passed Keegan's Gunsmiths [26] on Upper Ormond Quay and proceeded along the quay by the Four Courts. They had been detailed to escort five London and North Western wagons laden with munitions from the docks to the magazine in the Phoenix Park. As the Lancers proceeded along the quays, the troopers noticed armed men on the roofs of buildings. Hunter put out Trooper Arthur James Scarlett (No. 6297) as a forward scout. As the convoy reached the junction of Church Street and the quay, Volunteer Peadar Clancy's section at the barricade opened fire. Horses reared and plunged in fright as bullets cut through the air. Scarlett was shot dead and others were wounded as the Lancers wheeled the wagons around and attempted to get out of the line of fire.[1]

Hunter ordered his men to fall back and seek cover in the side-streets off the quays. As the Lancers fell back along the quay, Volunteers located in the Four Courts [3] building opened fire causing further casualties. Charging through the side-streets the troopers were blocked by the numerous barricades the Volunteers had erected. The Lancers fired wildly in all directions, accidentally killing a young girl. Hanging from their saddles, the wounded troopers wheeled around in circles and made easy targets for the Volunteers. Hunter rallied some of his men and ordered them to take cover in Collier's Dispensary [24] and the nearby Medical Mission, just off the quay on Charles Street. Dismounting, the Lancers hauled boxes of ammunition through the door, overturned the wagons to form a barricade and the troopers took up firing positions in the windows. Horses were cut loose and the riderless mounts ran wild, the sound of their hooves clattering along the cobbled streets.

At the upper end of Church Street, Volunteers Patrick Kelly and Phil Walsh were on guard duty. Looking down the street towards the sound of the shooting, Kelly saw a Lancer and a riderless horse coming towards their position. The Lancer leaned forward with his lance at the charge. Walsh fired but missed the moving target. The Lancer charged as Kelly prepared to fire. Commandant Daly appeared and ordered his men to hold their ground. Drawing his .45 revolver, he placed the weapon on Kelly's shoulder to steady his aim. Daly pulled the trigger and fired. The Lancer fell from the horse, mortally wounded. The Volunteers caught the terrified horses and sent them back in the direction of the quays in order to confuse any others that may be following. Daly ordered that any prisoners captured and the wounded were to be taken to the Father Matthew Hall [5]. The lance taken from the trooper was wedged into a manhole at the Junction of Church St and North King Street. A tricolour was then attached and the Volunteers raised their weapons and fired a salute over the banner.

It was believed that a number of Lancers had taken refuge within the Bridewell police station [29], located behind the Four Courts. Volunteer Section Commander Michael O'Flanagan was ordered to take a section of men and thoroughly search the building. The Volunteers approached the front of the building and blew the locks of the door. They entered the main hall and found saddles, bridles and loaded rifles. A further search discovered two Lancers in a cell in one of the blocks. The two troopers were then marched under guard to the Four Courts. A further search of the basement cells uncovered 23 members of the Dublin Metropolitan Police. They were ordered out in single file with their hands above their heads and removed under guard to the Four Courts for interrogation. Searches of the building resulted in a cache of arms and ammunition. The station sergeant stated that two civilian prisoners were held in the cells. These prisoners, a man and a woman who had been arrested on drunk and disorderly charges the previous Saturday, were released.

***

At 12.00 hours on Easter Monday 24th April 1916, the British contingent at the Royal Barracks [13] (National Museum, Collins Barracks) received an urgent communiqué from garrison headquarters at Dublin Castle. It ordered all troops in barracks to proceed to the castle fully armed. The 10th Royal Dublin Fusiliers was stationed at the Royal Barracks under the command of Lieutenant-Colonel Grattan Esmonde. At this time the regiment consisted of 37 officers and 430 other ranks. The inlying picquet of the Battalion made ready and at 12.30 hours a column of British soldiers marching four deep left the barracks and proceeded along the north quays on their way to Dublin Castle. No scouts or advance guard preceded the column and as they came in line with the Mendicity [2] at Ellis's Street and Blackhall Place two shots rang out in rapid succession. If Captain Seán Heuston in the Mendicity blew his whistle its sound was lost as the Volunteers unleashed a barrage of fire on the British contingent. Taken completely by surprise the British soldiers sought cover and returned fire. Lieutenant Gerald Neilan of the Royal Dublin Fusilers was shot through the head and died instantaneously. Nine other ranks were wounded. Neilan had only transferred to the Fusiliers in February 1916. A native of Ballygalda, Roscommon, he was 34 years old and unmarried.

With the shrill blast of a whistle, the British soldiers withdrew from the quay and disappeared into the side-streets, away from the range of the guns of Heuston's men. All went silent. The Volunteers in the Mendicity reloaded their weapons and made ready.

The next move came from the Queen Street direction. Exiting from the rear gate of the barracks, via Arbour Hill and Queen Street, a strong force of British troops moved out using the houses and side-streets to cover their approach to the quay. Within a short time a large concentration of men had taken up position without the Irish Volunteers' knowledge. Machine-gun fire from a Lewis gun was directed on to the Mendicity Institute.

Bullets ricocheted off the walls of the building forcing the Volunteers to take cover. The remaining glass in the window frames shattered and bullets became imbedded in the walls of the rooms. Expecting an attack on his position, Heuston ordered his men to prepare for an assault. The young officer and Volunteer Patrick Stephenson moved out onto the landing and crawled into a room that overlooked Queen Street Bridge [23]. With their weapons at the ready and two canister bombs they waited for an assault through the courtyard gate.

However, the suppression fire that was directed against Heuston's men was not a preparation for an attack but was covering fire that enabled 130 British soldiers under the command of Major M.A. Tighe to run the gauntlet across Queen Street Bridge and up Watling Street and on towards Dublin Castle. The Volunteers watched as steel-helmeted figures dashed across the bridge. The British soldiers succeeded in crossing the bridge and soon arrived at Ship Street Barracks in the Castle, reinforcing the small garrison within its walls. The threat of an assault on the Mendicity faded and the small garrison cleaned their weapons and made ready.

At 12.30 hours a telephone message was received at the Curragh Army Camp in County Kildare requesting military assistance in Dublin city. A mobile column consisting of the 3rd Reserve Cavalry Brigade travelled by train to Kingsbridge Station, just over a kilometre from the Volunteer's positions, arriving at 16.15 hours.

Battalion headquarters were established in the director's office in the train station and soldiers and officers made ready to move out. A company of men were immediately entrained to the North Wall via the loop-line, passing under the Phoenix

Park, continuing on by the Old Cabra Road to Glasnevin, then along the Royal Canal by Cross Guns Bridge, Binns Bridge, Jones's Road, Summerhill arriving at the North Wall. The troops then moved out, occupying Amiens Street Station and the Custom House. Snipers were positioned in the clock tower of Dublin Castle and ordered to cover the north quays near the Four Courts. The British were establishing a firm foothold in order to begin their campaign to regain control of Dublin city.

Chapter 4

Easter Monday 24 April 1916: Evening

By nightfall the Irish Volunteers were entrenched in their positions in the Four Courts [3] and the surrounding area. Barricades and roadblocks controlled the traffic in and out of the district.

Throughout the day many people attempted to get through the roadblocks that had been erected all over Dublin city by the Volunteers. A motor car approaching the Church Street Bridge [1] roadblock failed to stop when challenged. Lieutenant Peadar Clancy and his section opened fire on the vehicle wounding the driver and his passengers. The occupants of the vehicle, Lord Dunsany (the noted playwright) and a Colonel Lindsay, were officers in the Inniskilling Fusiliers and were trying to make their way towards their regimental headquarters at Amiens Street. Both men and their wounded chauffeur were taken prisoner and led towards the Father Matthew Hall [5]. As they were being led away, the Volunteer Captain stated that there was 'no danger of them entering *The Glittering Gates* just yet', alluding to a play by Lord Dunsany that had been popular at the Abbey theatre. Dunsany congratulated himself having been captured by literary men.[1]

At approximately 21.30 hours a coach turned in to May Lane from Bow Street. It was driven by John Murray of Messrs. A O'Neill & Son. Having collected a party from the Fairyhouse Races, Murray dropped them at Inchicore and was returning the coach to the depot on the North Strand. The driver, unaware of the situation in the area, galloped headlong into a group of Volunteers manning a roadblock. The order to halt was shouted, but whether the driver chose to ignore the command or did not hear the call, Murray was mortally wounded as a fusillade of shots was fired at the coach. Murray was 40 years old and left a wife and six children. His wife was to die only 4 years later, leaving the children orphaned.

Many civilians had been unable to return to their homes, and those fleeing from the day's events took refuge at the Richmond Hospital [15]. The Volunteers had attempted to take charge of the hospital but the staff objected strongly. The discussion became heated and Dr Joe O'Carroll advised residents not to cooperate with the Volunteers. He was threatened and had a revolver put to his head. The doctor stated that military personnel of either side taking possession of the building would put the patients and civilians in danger. After a long debate the Volunteers chose not to occupy the building and withdrew their force back to Brunswick Street.

Communication between Volunteer Headquarters at the General Post Office in Sackville Street and the Four Courts was carried out by Volunteers Ignatious Callender and Joseph Reynolds of the Fianna Éireann and Catherine Rooney of the

Cumann na mBan. Running the gauntlet of British sniper fire, these three Volunteers carried despatches between Commandant Daly and Volunteer Commander-in-Chief, Patrick Pearse. Volunteer reinforcements were promised to the Four Courts garrison and Daly reported back the disposition of British troops west of the General Post Office. The Rising was going according to plan and morale among the men was high.

It was on Church Street that the Irish Volunteers suffered their first casualty. Volunteer Edward J. Costello was shot in the head by sniper fire. Stretcher-bearers carried his body under a Red Cross flag to Jervis Street Hospital [10] where he died soon after. He held the rank of Second Lieutenant in the Irish Volunteers and was 19 years old. He was married and was a resident of Kilcock in County Kildare.

By late evening Daly's command had increased considerably as Volunteers had heard of the mobilisation order and had reported for duty. The street lamps were extinguished, leaving the streets in darkness. Daly and Béasalí toured the positions and ensured that sentries were relieved at regular intervals.

'Reilly's Fort' [21] was located at the junction of North King Street and Church Street. This post was used as a respite area for those coming off guard duty. This central location was garrisoned by a small section commanded by Lieutenant Jack Shouldice. On arriving at this fortified public house, the men coming off duty were fed and many managed to bed down for a few hours' sleep. Sentry duty was arranged – four hours on and four hours off.[2] Anybody approaching one of the barricades was challenged and asked for the password in order to pass. Throughout the night the sound of desultory firing could be heard from the centre of the city.

***

The British High Command in Ireland issued a communiqué via the naval base at Kingstown (now Dún Laoghaire) requesting reinforcements from the War Office in London in order to suppress an armed uprising. On Monday evening 24th April 1916, the 59th North Midland Division under the command of Major-General A.E. Sandbach, C.B., D.S.O., received orders from Brigade headquarters to 'stand to' for an immediate move. Recruited from the many towns and villages in the North of England, the 59th North Midland Division was a mobile division consisting of a number of regiments still in training. The soldiers had volunteered for action and had come from a variety of professions such as coalmining, law, retail and many from the slums of northern England. They had been nicknamed 'The Lost Divison' as they had lost any hope of heading to France. The division consisted of three brigades: 176th (2/5th, 2/6th South Staffordshire regiment, 2/5th, 2/6th North Staffordshire regiment); 177th (2/4th, 2/5th Lincolnshire regiment, 2/4th, 2/5th Leicestershire regiment) and the 178th infantry division (2/5th, 2/6th, 2/7th and 2/8th Battalions of the Sherwood Forester regiment).[3]

Many men had obtained leave for the holiday weekend and as they returned to barracks they were informed of the impending move. Soldiers from each battalion were furnished with 48 hours' dry rations and a quantity of ammunition. The men were enthusiastic at the thought of active service overseas and believed that a critical situation had developed on the Western Front and that the 59th division was destined for France or Flanders. They were very mistaken.

Chapter 5

Tuesday 25 April 1916

At 00.00 hours in England, the North and South Battalions of the Staffordshire regiments mobilised from their base at St Albans, Hertfordshire. These young men had been recruited from the industrial heartland of Britain's 'Black Country'. They were Volunteers who had left behind the pitheads, slag heaps, forging and smelting yards to fight for King and Country. With only 6 weeks of basic training completed, many of the men believed they were on their way to the Western Front. The companies were fully up to strength and every man was enthusiastic with the idea of active service after many months of waiting and so many false alarms.[1]

The troops entrained from Boxmoor Station to Liverpool at 03.45 hours on Tuesday morning. At this time the destination of the regiments was unknown to both officers and men, but on arriving at the train station they read the newspaper placards announcing a rebellion in Ireland. The Staffordshire (176th)

Brigade under Brigadier General L.R. Carleton D.S.O. was ferried across the Irish Sea in relays by two regular cross-channel boats, escorted by destroyers as German submarines were suspected in the locality. By late on Tuesday evening the Staffordshire regiment had disembarked in Dublin. Some of the men were under the impression that they had arrived in France. One of them, after seeing a number of civilians on the quayside, was heard to remark, 'I say, Bill, they've picked up our language pretty quick!'

The men were billeted in a disused hotel. It was to be early on Wednesday morning, though, before all the troops had assembled at Kingstown.

As British forces landed in Ireland, an attempted breakthrough to reinforce Dublin Castle by Crown forces took place. Early on Tuesday morning six transport wagons under mounted escort made their way along the south quay. As they came abreast to Church Street Bridge [1], Volunteer Lieutenant Peader Clancy ordered his men to open fire. Convoy riders tumbled from their mounts, as bullets tore into their horses. The only way the British force could extract itself from this predicament was to about turn and return back down the quays. With the convoy under intense fire, the Volunteers watched as the wagons turned and galloped back towards the Royal Barracks [13]. As the shooting stopped, Clancy and his men walked across the bridge and collected five rifles and 1,000 rounds of ammunition.

At 04.00 hours Brigadier General Lowe, commanding the Reserve Cavalry Brigade from the Curragh, arrived in Kingsbridge Station (now Heuston Station). Accompanying him were 1,000 troops of the 25th Irish Infantry Brigade. Lowe took immediate command of the situation in the absence of the Commander-in-Chief, Major-General C.B. Friend, who was on holiday. In order to relieve and secure Dublin Castle, Colonel Portal was ordered to establish a line of posts from Kingsbridge Station to Trinity College via the Castle. This course of action would divide the positions of the Irish Volunteers, north and south of the River Liffey, enabling Crown forces to establish a safe line of advance and of communication. They could then extend operations to the north and south of the city.

At the Mendicity Institute [2] Captain Heuston ordered Volunteer John MacLoughlin to make his way to the Volunteer GHQ at the General Post Office (GPO) to see James Connolly. In order to continue holding the Mendicity, food and reinforcements were needed urgently. MacLoughlin scaled the outer wall and disappeared into the early morning mist.

That morning, Commandant Daly moved his command post to the Father Matthew Hall [5] in Church Street in order to be in the centre of the Battalion zone. A number of Volunteers carried boxes of ammunition and explosives from the Convent of St John [22] to the Hall. As soon as the command post was established, Daly ventured out and inspected the positions. The commandant instructed Volunteer Lieutenant Liam O'Carroll to reinforce all the defences in the area. O'Carroll observed a mob of people trying to force their way into Monk's Bakery [19]. The Lieutenant detailed two Volunteers to guard the bakery and told those queueing that anyone who was willing to assist the Volunteers in reinforcing the barricades would be given bread. A number of men came forward and O'Carroll directed them to take materials from a building site on Church Street opposite the Father Matthew Hall and follow him.[2]

At noon on Tuesday, the 4th Royal Dublin Fusiliers from Templemore, a composite Ulster Battalion and a battery of four 18-pounder guns from the Reserve Artillery Brigade in Athlone, arrived in Dublin. The gun battery detrained at Blanchardstown and moved by road towards Phibsborough. A firing position for the guns was set up at the Medical Officers' Residency in Grangegorman Asylum. A strong force of British infantry from the 4th Battalion of the Royal Dublin Fusiliers moved out from the Phoenix Park towards the Volunteer positions at the Cabra Road and North Circular Road barricade.

At 15.45 hours a shrapnel shell burst over the barricade showering the Volunteers with hot debris. The 30 men of 'B' Company of the Irish Volunteers took cover as the shells exploded. Under the cover of the artillery barrage the British infantry moved up and opened fire on the barricade. The Volunteers held on with great tenacity. For the next three-quarters of an hour shell after shell rained down on their position. The Fusiliers fought a running battle with the Volunteers along the railway line between Broadstone up to the Cabra Bridge. Volunteer John Cromien was killed in action in this area. Employed as a number-taker at the Guinness Brewery, John Cromien was 23 years old when he was shot dead. Attempts by the Volunteers to destroy the Cabra Bridge and the bridge crossing the Midland Railwayline on the North Circular Road were unsuccessful. Under this intense artillery fire, Volunteer Captain James Sullivan decided to extricate his men from the position and ordered a withdrawal from the post. Leaving a small rearguard to cover his withdrawal, Sullivan and his men withdrew towards Glasnevin. Later, some of his men managed to link up with Commandant Thomas Ashe's 5th Battalion in North county Dublin.[3] The rearguard was taken prisoner after a brief gun battle and escorted to Richmond military barracks. With the fall of the Volunteer positions the British had managed to establish a cordon around the northern part of the city from Parkgate Street, along the North Circular Road to the North Wall. The city had been surrounded and the Volunteers cut off. The planned line of retreat northwards for the Irish Volunteer forces had been eradicated.

Back at his command post Daly realised that there were two immediate threats to his position. The first was Broadstone Railway Station [12] and the second was Linenhall Army Barracks [6]. The station dominated Constitution Hill and looked down on his battalion zone. If occupied by Crown forces, they would hold the high ground and dominate the area. Daly ordered a unit of twelve Volunteers under the command of Captain Denis O'Callaghan to reconnoitre the station to determine if it was occupied and what the enemy's strength in that complex was. If they found the building empty they were to occupy and hold the position. Sergeant Peadar Breslin ordered the men to draw rations from the quartermaster and make ready to move out. At noon, the unit moved out in single file and proceeded up Constitution Hill and Nugents Lane towards the station.

Taking the point position, Volunteer Garry Holohan led the men, with Eamon Martin half way between him and the main party. As Holohan came near the building he noticed a figure running across the inside of the carriage entrance. He could not determine if it was a khaki or Volunteer uniform and signalled for the column to halt. Martin continued to move up in support and as he came abreast with Holohan a shot rang out hitting Martin. The Volunteer yelled out, 'Garry, I'm shot,' before collapsing.[4] A barrage of rifle fire then erupted from the building and bullets ricocheted off the ground around the two men. Holohan dragged his wounded comrade out of the line of fire and sought what little cover existed. A unit of the 4th Royal Dublin Fusiliers had moved up under the cover of darkness and had occupied the station. They directed sporadic rifle fire at O'Callaghan's Volunteers causing sparks to fly as bullets ricocheted off the cobbled street. The Volunteers took cover and returned fire. Chips of masonry were blown from the front of the building. The Volunteers could hear the shouting of orders and see, here and there, the figures of British infantry moving out from behind cover as their rifles and machine guns poured fire from the station. O'Callaghan ordered his men to fall back to Church Street. The Volunteers positioned in the high buildings beside Moore's Coach House and Clarke's Dairy [20] opened fire in order to cover the retreating Volunteers.

As they ran the gauntlet back to their own lines Volunteer George Butler turned, dropped to one knee and fired. He retreated another few yards, loaded his weapon and fired again and again. In full view of the enemy he repeated this covering action until he reached the safety of his own lines. Second Lieutenant George R. Gray of the Royal Dublin Fusiliers was shot dead as he took aim from a window in the station. Gray was aged 22, a dental student and the son of Alexander and Helen Gray, of Newcastle-on-Tyne. Martin was evacuated to the Richmond Hospital [15] suffering from a gunshot wound to the lung. O'Callaghan reported to Daly that he encountered determined opposition and had sustained casualties. Daly, realising that the British were entrenched in the building, abandoned the idea of another attack on the station. The Volunteers in Clarke's

Dairy and Moore's Coach House kept up a sustained fire at the station in order to deter the British from launching an attack from there.

Throughout the day, many Volunteers who had received the mobilisation order late on Monday reinforced the ranks of Commandant Daly's command. Reporting for the duty, the men, women and young boys were directed to their positions by Vice-Commandant Béaslaí.

Volunteer Mortimer O'Connell, who was on sentry duty near Smithfield, was ordered to scout out towards the Royal Barracks [13]. O' Connell reported back to Daly that large formations of troops were amassing in the area of the barracks. In order to deny the enemy a way of ingress towards the Volunteer positions on Church Street from the Smithfield direction it was decided to destroy a footbridge in Bow Street. This bridge linked the administrative part of the Jameson Distillery [8] to the distillery proper, and could provide the enemy with a foothold in the area. Running the gauntlet of sniper fire, Volunteers managed to place a number of canister bombs on the bridge. The Volunteers then opened fire on the bombs, hoping that the explosion would destroy the bridge. The bombs failed to explode, leaving the bridge intact and the threat of attack remaining.

Listening to the echo of sporadic rifle fire coming from the city, Heuston waited anxiously for the return of his scout to the Mendicity Institute. As he looked from his post he saw a group of Volunteers rushing towards the building over Queen Street Bridge [23]. Volunteer Macloughlin had managed to get through to the GHQ at the Post Office and was returning with a small detachment from the Swords Battalion under Lieutenant Dick Coleman. This brought Hueston's small garrison to 26.

Food was still in short supply, and whatever rations the Volunteers had were already gone. Heuston ordered MacLoughlin and Patrick Stephenson to make their way to GHQ at the General Post Office and get as much food as possible and report to command that they now intended to hold this position for as long as they could. Both Volunteers scaled the wall and disappeared into the night.

Chapter 6

Wednesday 26 April 1916: The Battle of the Mendicity

By 06.00 hours on Wednesday morning, in preparation for an assault on the Mendicity Institute [2], British soldiers began evacuating the occupants in the houses on each side of the complex. They then took up firing positions in the buildings on Thomas Street, Bonham Street, Watling Street and Bridgefoot Street, effectively cutting off and surrounding Captain Seán Heuston's position.

Having successfully delivered Heuston's message to Commandant James Connolly at GHQ in the General Post Office on Sackville Street (later O'Connell Street), Volunteers John MacLoughlin and Patrick Stephenson made their way back towards the Mendicity Institute.

At Queen Street Bridge [23] the men watched helplessly as British troops made ready for their assault. Cut off and unable to break through to their unit, the Volunteers made their way towards the Four Courts [3] in order to report the situation to Commandant Daly.

Heuston estimated that his small garrison of 26 was facing a force of 300-400 British troops. He attempted to send two other Volunteers with a despatch to Connolly at the GPO but the men returned having failed to break through the British lines.

At noon on Wednesday, the British launched their attack. The attack on their position was to be bitterly contested by the Volunteers. Soldiers from the Royal Dublin Fusiliers opened fire on Heuston's position at the Institute from all sides. Multiple machine-guns unleashed a torrent of fire from concealed positions on the opposite side of the River Liffey. Rapid independent fire from the Fusiliers saw the riflemen working their bolts with practised efficiency, firing at a steady rate of one round in less than four seconds. The windows at the Mendicity suddenly splintered and bullet holes ripped across the plaster. As the British advanced towards the Mendicity, the front of the building erupted in a sudden blast of flame as the Irish Volunteers opened a ragged fire that brought several of the advancing enemy down. Soon, the floor of the building was littered with empty brass shell casings. Heuston moved from room to room encouraging his men. As the battle developed, the shooting was frequently at close quarters. At times there was only a distance of 20 feet between combatants.

The suppression fire laid down by the machine-guns enabled Crown forces to move slowly along the quay wall until they reached the boundary wall at the front of the Mendicity. This manoeuvre brought them within a few feet of their quarry. The soldiers pulled pins from grenades and hurled them into the complex. Heuston's men grabbed at them frantically and threw them back over the wall at the British. Smoke and debris littered the rooms as the Volunteers fought desperately to repel the attackers. Explosions echoed throughout the streets and the shouts and groans from the wounded reverberated along the quays. One grenade rolled across the floor and exploded within the Mendicity, showering the defenders with shrapnel. Two Volunteers, Liam Staines and Dick Balfe, were badly injured.

Outnumbered, without food and short of ammunition, Heuston realised that in a short time his position would be over-run. Deliberating on these facts, the young officer consulted his men, telling them that the only option open to them was one of surrender. Many of his troops objected, but the order was reluctantly obeyed. The men destroyed their weapons and equipment. One of the Volunteers went out the rear door of the building carrying a white flag. The shooting stopped and an eerie silence descended on the area. The others followed, carrying their wounded comrades. As they crossed the yard towards the back gate at Island Street, a single shot rang out, killing Volunteer Peter Wilson. A native of Swords in county Dublin, Volunteer Peter Wilson was 40 years old.

On seeing the small force that had held them up and inflicted so many casualties among their ranks, the British were infuriated. They ordered the Volunteers to march to the Royal Barracks [13] (now Collins Barracks, National Museum of Ireland) with their hands held above their heads. The men who marched out of the Mendicity: Captain Séan Heuston, John Derrington, Liam Derrington, Tom Kelly, Joe Byrne, Frank Cullen, William O'Dea,

Liam Roche, W. Meehan, R. Kelly, J. Wilson, W. Wilson, J. Clarke, J. Marks, P. Wilson, R. Coleman, J. Corrigan, T. Peppard, J. Norton, P. Kelly, George Levins and Fred Brooks. The Volunteers had suffered one man killed in action and two wounded. The ages of the garrison, apart from one man of 40, ranged from 18 to 25 years.

Having initially been ordered to hold the position for a few hours, Heuston had held on for three days against overwhelming odds. Heuston's small unit had fought a desperate battle behind a barricade of sandbags deep inside their position. They had proved that, although the battlefield of Dublin would be dominated by artillery, human endeavour still counted.

Chapter 7

Wednesday 26 April 1916

On Wednesday morning, the newly arrived British regiments from England marched to the Royal Agricultural Grounds (RDS) in Ballsbridge via Blackrock. The 59th Division was on the verge of its baptism of fire, and in the last city of all cities in which it had been expected to be baptised – Dublin.[1] The people in the Dublin suburbs turned out *en masse* to greet the Brigade. From all sides offerings of oranges, bananas, sandwiches and chocolate were pressed on the men. Women walked beside the columns holding saucers as the soldiers drank cups of tea.

The regiments were halted, and the men of the Staffordshire battalions were instructed to load their weapons as resistance was expected on the road ahead. Many of the recruits had received little or no instruction in musketry and a few unintentional shots were discharged. Though this caused some alarm, order was soon restored. At the RDS, the Staffordshire Brigade under the command of Brigadier General Carlton were ordered to remain in reserve while the Sherwood Foresters advanced towards the city. At Mount Street Bridge, the Sherwood Foresters suffered heavy casualties in an engagement with the Irish Volunteers.[2]

Having successfully dealt with the Volunteer force in the Mendicity Institute [2], British troops began establishing defensive positions on the south quays of the River Liffey. Under the cover of a Red Cross ambulance, an artillery piece was moved into a firing position close to St Michael and John's Church on the south quay. The Volunteers could hear crow bars lifting the paving stones in order to fix the gun in position. It was decided to fire on the ambulance, forcing the vehicle to drive away in the direction of Capel Street. Two shells were fired from the gun, hitting the East Wing of the Courts building, exploding and showering the defenders with dust and debris. The Volunteers opened fire, forcing the gunners to take cover. The artillery shells that were fired were not effective on the walls of the Courts, and firing ceased soon after.[3]

A section of the Royal Dublin Fusiliers had occupied buildings on the opposite side of the river at Bridge Street and Ushers Quay. The British soldiers opened fire at the west wing of the Four Courts and at the barricade at Church Street Bridge [1]. Flashes of gunfire emanated from the windows forcing the Volunteers to take cover. Pinned down and unable to return fire, the Volunteers were in danger of an assault that could overrun their position.

It was vital that the British were dislodged from their position immediately. Lieutenant Peader Clancy and Tom Smart seized four cans of petrol and made their way across the bridge. Running between each section of the bridge, they paused to take cover as British troops fired desperately at the men. There was not a vestige of cover as Clancy and Smart made the final dash across the open street to the frontage of the buildings. Breaking the downstairs windows, they poured the petrol through and set it alight. Under rifle fire, the Volunteers turned and ran back across the bridge. The fire took hold and spread rapidly, forcing the British to evacuate. The four houses at Bridge Street and Ushers Quay burned fiercely, scorching the frontage of the historic Brazen Head Hotel.

With the threat of attack from both the north and south of his position repelled, Commandant Daly now turned his attention to Linenhall Barracks [6]. At 12.00 hours, Captain Denis O'Callaghan and a group of Volunteers made their way to the front gate of the barracks. They demanded the immediate surrender of the small British force inside. The garrison refused to surrender, and the Irish Volunteers, using canister bombs, attempted to breach the wall. This did not succeed, but the tremendous explosion caused the British to re-examine the proposal. Eventually, the main gate was opened and they surrendered.

The Volunteers captured 32 unarmed Pay Corp clerks and a policeman. They were led off at gunpoint to the Father Matthew Hall [5]. The Volunteers did not have enough manpower to occupy this complex, and it was decided that the barracks should be destroyed. O'Callaghan and Garry Holohan brought paints and oils from Moore's druggist's shop [28] in North King Street. On the first floor of the barracks, the men piled up the bed boards and spilled the contents of a number of barrels onto floor. They then lit the fire. The fire spread rapidly, and both men found it difficult to evacuate the building. On returning from the Father Matthew Hall, where he had been ordered to take the prisoners, Volunteer Patrick Kelly wrote,

I returned from the Father Matthew Hall about an hour later and by that time the barracks was a roaring furnace. To the front of the barracks was a block of tenement houses. They were in danger of becoming alight and that, had it occurred, would have rendered our positions untenable. We procured a hose and standpipe from the North Dublin Union. We played water on the front of the houses and prevented the fire spreading in our direction. During the night the fire had spread in an easterly direction and involved Hugh Moore and Alexander's, wholesale druggists' premises, where large stores of oils and inflammable goods became ignited. Barrels of oil and spirits burst occasionally and sent flames, with a loud explosion, hundreds of feet into the air. The entire neighbourhood was as bright as day.[4]

This fire was to continue burning over the next four days.

In order to try and get bread for their families, many of the local populace ran the gauntlet of fire in order to get to Monk's Bakery [19]. On being stopped at the barricades, many of the women became abusive and had to be threatened at the point of a Volunteer bayonet. Some of the Volunteers let the women through the barricades until they were ordered to stop, question and search all those attempting to get through. Suspicions had been aroused as a number of British soldiers and police officers dressed as women were trying to gain information on the strength of the Volunteers in the area.

At the Four Courts, the Volunteers were under constant fire from the Lancers who had taken refuge in the Medical Mission on Charles Street on Monday. The Lancers, knowing that they could not expect a re-supply, conserved their ammunition, rations and water carefully. The conditions in which they had continued to fight since Monday were terrible. They were choked with smoke and dust from the battle. They were willing to fight to the last round and to the last man. Strained by exhaustion as much as battle shock they held on to their position. The windows of the Medical Mission looked out towards the Chancery Place [27] entrance to the Four Courts. In an exchange of gunfire, the officer commanding the Lancers, Second Lieutenant G.J. Hunter, was shot dead.

The Volunteers decided to launch an attack on the Medical Mission in order to drive out the Lancers and capture the ammunition. From the Chancery Place gate of the Four Courts, the Volunteers laid down a covering fire against the Mission. Two Volunteers dashed across the road and flung a makeshift incendiary device through the window. It failed to ignite the building. As the men turned to make their way back, the Lancers opened fire, hitting Volunteer Paddy Daly. He slumped to the ground as he neared the Chancery Gate. The Volunteers rushed forward to retrieve the stricken Daly and hauled the injured man into the building. Daly was taken to the improvised hospital in the Four Courts where his wounds were dressed. The Lancers still held their position.

British marksmen had taken up sniping positions in the tower of Christ Church Cathedral, Powers Distillery tower and the Bermingham tower in Dublin Castle. New skills in long-range shooting and camouflage had been learnt and practised on the Western Front in Europe. A skilful sniper could not only cause casualties but also lower the morale of his enemy. By holding the roofs of high buildings, the British dominated the battleground giving them the best fields of fire.

A machine-gun located on the roof of Jervis Street hospital [10] opened fire on the Volunteer positions. This rooftop had a commanding view of the battle zone. Machine-gun fire knocked up dust as Volunteers ran in short rushes from point to point. Many men sustained minor injuries and had to be evacuated to the Red Cross Station at the Father Matthew Hall. The British machine-gunner on the roof traversed his weapon and emptied drum after drum of ammunition in to the Irish positions. The Volunteers at the Malt House Tower [31] in Beresford Street managed to get a powerful set of binoculars. The spotter, using the eyeglasses, located the machine-gunner on the roof and informed Lieutenant Frank Shouldice. Taking up his sniping position, Shouldice took careful aim at the British gunner. Squeezing the trigger of his rifle, he emptied the magazine into the British position, killing the gunner and firing ceased from the target building.[5]

On the Smithfield side of the battlefield, soldiers of the Royal Dublin Fusiliers set up a machine-gun position and opened fire on the west wing of the Four Courts. The west wall became torn and pitted as bullets smashed into the edifice, splintering window-frames and shattering glass. Volunteer Thomas Allen was hit and killed as he held the Record Office in the complex. The machine-gun fire was so intense that Father O'Callaghan and Father Augustine had to crawl along the floor in order to reach the dying Volunteer and give him absolution. Thomas Allen was 30 years old, attached to 'C' Company of the 1st Battalion and was a native of County Meath. His death left a widow and four children.

Gun battles continued throughout the night. At approximately 23.00 hours, a section of Volunteers that included

Patrick Kelly, Louis McEvatt and John McCormack made their way towards the avenue leading to the North Dublin Union [14]. They were ordered to guard the flank of the Battalion's command. Illuminated by the fire at the Linenhall barracks, the men made their way past darkened, skeletal buildings towards their post. Halfway to their destination, they had to cross an exposed piece of ground that was illuminated by the barrack fire. The British, positioned at the North Dublin Union, took advantage of the illumination, and as the Volunteers crossed the patch of ground they were pinned down under sustained rifle and heavy machine-gun fire. They threw themselves on the ground and crawled for cover. Heavy fire erupted between both sides. As the gun battle intensified, the authorities in the Union pleaded with both sides not to use the grounds as it endangered the people who had taken refuge within the complex. After some time the firing ceased and both sides withdrew their forces from the grounds.

That night, both sides kept alert, listening to the dull crack of a sniper's rifle, the odd burst of machine-gun fire and the distant whistle of a signal flare going up. The tide was slowly beginning to turn against the Volunteers.

Chapter 8

Thursday 27 April 1916

At 00.30 hours on Thursday morning, the Staffordshire Regiment moved up the line to Northumberland Road and were billeted in Beggars Bush Barracks, Ballsbridge. A detachment was sent out to relieve the Sherwood Foresters, who, having taken the Irish Volunteer positions at Mount Street Bridge, were occupying strategic buildings in the locality. They spent until dawn under continuous sniper fire from Irish Volunteer positions at Boland's Mills. Later that morning, the Staffordshire regiment advanced to Trinity College, where they reinforced the college garrison and awaited further orders. At 04.30 hours, the 2/5th of the Sherwood Foresters were despatched from the Royal Hospital at Kilmainham to reinforce Kingsbridge Station. The 2/6th Sherwood Foresters were ordered to Dublin Castle. There, they billeted in the castle yard and were told to await further orders.

By 12.00 hours on Thursday, British reinforcements were pouring into Dublin city. Brigadier General W.H.M. Lowe had almost 16,000 troops at his disposal. Major-General Friend returned from abroad to assume overall command of British ground forces in Ireland. Lowe briefed him on the situation and his plan to retake the city. By means of fighting patrols, Lowe had gathered information in relation to the strengths and disposition of the Irish Volunteers. His plans consisted of raising a cordon around the city isolating the Volunteer GHQ at the GPO, and also Daly's command at the Four Courts [3]. By concentrating his forces there, General Lowe could destroy the control point of the Rising.

Using Trinity College as a base of operations in the city, British forces had established a number of posts that ran from College Green on towards Tara Street, Gardiner Street, Parnell Street, by Broadstone Railway Station [12], to North Brunswick Street and on to Kingsbridge Railway Station. On the south side of the River Liffey, troops were in position from Dame Street, Christ Church, Thomas Street and linked up at Kingsbridge Railway Station. However, there was a gap on the north side of the city in the line from Parnell Street to Kingsbridge Station. Lowe's strategy was to connect the two positions, and he planned that part of this cordon on the north side of the city would connect at North King Street. To begin this part of his operation he needed to gain a foothold in the area.

In order to move freely in the area, two improvised Armoured Personnel Carriers (APCs) had been built in the previous afternoon at the Inchicore Railway Works. A retired Colonel of the Royal Irish Rifles named Henry T. W. Allatt devised the idea of fitting two flat-bed Daimler lorries with large boilers that had been supplied by the Guinness Brewery. In order to protect the driver, the cab of the lorry had been armoured with heavy steel plating. He was able to drive the vehicle by looking through a small slit in the plating. Loop-holes were drilled in the sides of the boiler on the lorry-bed, providing firing slits for the troops in the back. A large slit cut into the back door was used as a firing point for a Lewis machine-gun. Each vehicle was capable of transporting 20 men.

At 17.00 hours, the first units of the 2/6th Battalion Sherwood Foresters moved out from Dublin Castle. Their objective was to secure and occupy Capel Street. As they prepared to cross Grattan Bridge, the area was swept with gunfire from Irish Volunteers at the Four Courts. Bullets struck the bridge, ricocheting against the balustrades, sending sparks and debris flying. In order to cover the advancing British units, an armoured personnel carrier deposited 16 riflemen into the church yard in St Michael's and St John's Church on the south quay. They took up position behind the tombstones, and opened fire at the Four Courts. Another group of soldiers took up position at the quay wall near the Adam and Eve Church [25], and opened fire across the river at the Four Courts. Back at the bridgehead, officers regrouped their men and then began advancing by alternate platoon rushes, covering the distance of the bridge.

Each company of the Sherwood Foresters was allocated a fixed area to clear, and each platoon or section was then assigned a building or street to secure in that area. Captain Edmunds with 'A' Company secured a sector from Capel Street to Coles Lane, while 'C' Company, under Captain Jackson, was made responsible for securing Upper Abbey and Liffey Streets. 'D' Company, under the command of Captain Tomkins, was ordered to secure the area from Coles Lane to Sackville Street and Captain Orr, commanding 'B' Company, was ordered to contain the Four Courts building.

The armoured cars drove at speed into Capel Street, and the operation commenced. As the vehicles drew to a halt, British troops debussed rapidly, taking up firing positions on the street while others kicked in front doors and entered buildings. They systematically began clearing tenement houses, shops and businesses. The structures were swept from front to back and from bottom to top. Gunfire exploded from inside and echoed throughout the streets. Terrified residents were kept under armed guard or forcibly removed from the area of operation. Sniper fire erupted, and a vicious shootout between Irish Volunteers and British forces broke out. The Sherwood Foresters battled from building to building, firing at an unseen enemy. In order to secure the area, British troops erected sandbag barricades at both ends of the street. Empty sacks were commandeered from a local factory and filled with earth from the floors of the many tenement houses in the area. Within a short period of time, the Sherwood Foresters had driven a wedge between the Volunteer GHQ at the GPO and Commandant Daly's Command at the Four Courts. Sporadic rifle fire continued, but the British had secured a firm foothold in the area.

The next course of action was to extricate the Lancers in the Medical Mission and at Collier's dispensary [24] on Chancery Place [27]. The Volunteers watched in astonishment as the improvised armoured cars drew to a halt and backed up to the door of the mission. The Volunteers opened fire on the armoured car. Bullets pinged off the metalwork as the Lancers loaded their dead officer, their wounded and the boxes of ammunition into the back of the car. This action was carried out a few times until the Lancers and the consignment of ammunition were safe.

Volunteer Joseph Reynolds was instructed by Daly to reconnoitre the area east of the Courts and try and discover what was happening in the Capel Street district. In order to gain as much cover as possible, Reynolds moved out making his way through the grounds of unfinished houses, through workshops and tenement yards until he had no choice but to take to the streets. As he moved along, the detritus of the Rising lay all around: rubble, the fragments of walls and shell casings were mixed with the wreckage of family houses, iron bedsteads, lamps and household utensils. Reynolds watched from cover as British soldiers pushed their way in to Bolton Street from Capel Street. Returning to Daly's Command Post, he reported that British troops had taken control of the area and were erecting barricades. Daly gave the Volunteer an urgent despatch for Patrick Pearse at GHQ. He urged the Volunteer to do his best to break through the British line and deliver the despatch as it was of the utmost importance. Reynolds once again made his way out of the area towards the General Post Office in Sackville Street. It took the Volunteer almost two hours to break through the cordon and deliver the despatch to Pearse. He also informed the Commander-in-Chief of the disposition of the British troops in the area. Reynolds then made the hazardous return journey back to Daly's command.

Volunteer Michael Flanagan was ordered to take his section and reinforce the small garrison that was holding Reilly's Fort [21] on North King Street. Sniper fire was intense, but Flanagan managed to report to Reilly's without suffering any casualties. He reported to the post commander, Lieutenant Maurice Collins, who directed the men to the upper windows of the building. The field of fire covered North King Street up as far as Bolton Street.

Sniper fire in the area intensified. The Bermingham Tower in Dublin Castle had been draped in large sheets of canvas in order to provide cover for British snipers. One British soldier was credited with more than 20 hits before he was shot. Volunteer Michael O'Dea was seriously wounded as he relieved Seán Byrne from sentry duty. A single shot hit O'Dea's rifle butt and then ricocheted, wounding him in both thighs and the abdomen. He was taken to the Red Cross station in the Father Matthew Hall [5], where his wounds were dressed and he was placed in a bed.[1] Captain Nicholas Laffan was also seriously wounded and evacuated from Moore's Coach Works. The young Fianna officer, Patrick Holohan was placed in command of Clarke's Dairy [20] and Moore's Coach Works [18].

Catherine Rooney of the Cumann na mBan made her way to Clarke's Dairy with bandoliers of ammunition. Volunteers were positioned on the top floor, surveying Broadstone Station [12] through field glasses. She asked permission to have a look. As she looked through the binoculars, bullets flew through the window and became embedded in a door. The men asked Catherine if she was injured as the missiles went very close to her head. She took off her beret and found two holes, the entry and exit point of the bullet. She was uninjured, and returned to duty carrying ammunition to the other posts.[2]

Towards 00.00 hours, Daly realised that his position was slowly being surrounded. He held a meeting with his officers and discussed the possibility of organising an attack on Crown forces positioned between the courts area and the GPO. Owing to the illumination created by the blaze at Linenhall barracks [6], and the small number of men that could be mustered for such an attack, the operation was cancelled. Officers were warned to expect heavy fighting in the next few hours. Extra supplies of grenades and ammunition were brought to 'Reilly's Fort' and Clarke's Dairy. The officers returned to their posts, and waited for the impending attack. They would not have to wait long.

Chapter 9

Friday 28 April 1916

At 02.00 hours, General Sir John Grenfell Maxwell KCB KCMG, general officer commanding British forces in Ireland, arrived by battleship at the North Wall Quay. He was immediately transferred to British Army headquarters at the Royal Hospital in Kilmainham. There, General Lowe briefed him of the plan to retake Dublin city. The 177th Brigade were to be divided, with the 2/5th and 2/6th South Staffordshire regiment being ordered to move across the River Liffey towards the Four Courts [3]. The remainder of Carleton's 177th Brigade was to contain De Valera's Volunteers at Boland's Bakery in Ballsbridge.

The 2/6th Battalion of the South Staffordshire Regiment under the command of Lieutenant-Colonel Henry Taylor now moved across the River Liffey and into action. Having been ordered to seal the cordon around the Four Courts, the battalion was ordered to advance westwards along North King Street and to link up with the 2/5th South Staffordshire Regiment pressing eastwards from Bridgefoot Street and over Queen Street Bridge [23]. Their regimental history describes the area:

> Few visitors to Dublin and not all of its inhabitants are deeply interested in North King Street. From a spectacular point of view in peacetime it was of little account, consisting as it did of innumerable houses of the smaller kind, and shops of a cheaper sort. If it was not actually a slum, it may certainly be described as a congested area, penetrated by infinite passages and alleys and more nearly resembling a rabbit warren than a battlefield.[1]

Unknown to Taylor, the 1st Battalion of the Irish Volunteers held North King Street.

An armoured personnel carrier screeched to a halt outside the Bolton Street Technical College [9], and a group of soldiers rushed up the steps and took control of the school. Many of the refugees were permitted to stay as Taylor established a command post.

Snipers took up position on the roof of the school, defensive barricades were erected on Bolton Street, and two houses were occupied at the junction of North King Street and Bolton Street by 'A' Company North Staffs. These houses were to be used as a staging area for the coming operation. Locals were questioned in order to garner intelligence on Volunteer positions and strengths. Taylor despatched a section from 'C' Company to North King Street. They advanced along the roadway in extended file, weapons at the ready.

On their right side, about 150 yards along the roadway, lay Coleraine Street, with Langan's Public House [7] on its corner with North King Street. A barricade stretched across this street, covered by a section of Volunteers in the public house. As the British soldiers came abreast of the street, they halted briefly as they were surprised to find the barricade unmanned. As the officer ordered his men to continue, a volley of rifle fire erupted from the windows of Langan's. Soldiers collapsed as a hail of bullets hit them. Lieutenant J. Sheppard was shot and mortally wounded in the first volley of fire. A civilian medical officer, who left cover in order to administer aid to the stricken officer, was shot dead. Another volley of fire from Reilly's public house [21] caused the British to fall back in disarray. Bullets ricocheted around them as they sought to get out of the line of fire. The soldiers were still battling as they turned in to an alleyway desperately seeking refuge. Every doorway, window and rooftop was a potential threat. Crossing through the alley, the remnants of the platoon entered Beresford Street, and into the sights of Frank Shouldice's men on the Jameson Granary Tower [31]. A fusillade of shots scattered the soldiers forcing them towards the partly built cottages backing on to Beresford Street and Stirrup Lane. As the British soldiers came in to range, a wave of rifle fire burst in front of the soldiers, practically wiping out the remainder of the platoon. The Volunteers, occupying the cottages, moved out from cover in order to collect the rifles and ammunition of the dead men. They got 100 rounds of ammunition, but the rifles had been shattered by the ferocity of the fire and were useless. The firing ceased, except for the occasional report from the snipers on the roof of the Technical School.

There was breathing space for about an hour before the next British assault was made. Two platoons from 'C' Company, supported by machine-gun fire, cautiously advanced up North King

Street. A heavy volume of covering fire was directed into Langan's Public House. The Volunteers Thomas Sheerin, William Murphy, John Williamson and John Dwan crouched for cover behind the window-sills as machine-gun bullets tore into the building. Within minutes, the building resembled a sieve; rubble was piled high on the floors, laths hung down from the ceilings and a fine, white dust covered everything. The Volunteers returned fire on their attackers and a vicious gun battle commenced. Supporting fire was received from the other Volunteer posts on North King Street. Some of the fire hit the British troops, and many fell, wounded or dead, but the majority pressed on with little hesitation. The small garrison in 'Reilly's Fort' opened fire on the advancing British troops, killing and wounding many. The British sent up another two platoons in support of the attackers. They were repulsed after heavy fighting.

Reilly's Fort, at the junction of North King Street and Church Street, commanded a stretch of road almost 200 yards long. British spotters identified this position as a possible threat from a tricolour flag that hung defiantly from a lance outside the building. Machine-gun fire was directed onto the building. Bullets stormed along the roof and inside the rooms, splashing clouds of yellow chips from the planking and plaster. The Volunteers were soon covered in a pale powder, giving them a spectral air. Lieutenant Jack Shouldice and his men returned a rapid fire from the barricaded windows. Empty shell casings flew through the guns' ejection ports and tumbled down, littering the floor. The battles were furious, and attack after attack was abandoned. Each time the British fell back, dragging their dead and wounded.

It was dangerous to expose oneself at any window or doorway. Sniper fire continued throughout the area. Duels were fought between Irish Volunteers and British soldiers. As a British officer moved down Prebend Street from the Broadstone Station [12], he was shot by a Volunteer sniper in Moore's Coach works. However, not all the casualties were military. One of the bakers who had spent the week working at Monk's Bakery opened the door in an attempt to leave for home. He was shot dead. British troops fired indiscriminately into houses on each side of the street. Many innocent civilians were trapped in their homes, terrified by the approaching gunfire.

***

The afternoon dissolved in sound. The din was hideous. The heavy boom of the Mauser rifles mixed with the high-pitched report from the British Lee Enfields. The cries of the wounded, punctuated by the sharp explosions of grenades, echoed throughout the streets. In the distance, the staccato sound of machine-guns intertwined with the boom of artillery fire. The Volunteers fought off successive British assaults throughout the day. The carefully prepared battleground was perfect for defence. The architecture of the area made locating and trapping the insurgents difficult. North King Street had been turned into a sophisticated death-trap.

In an attempt to outflank the barricade, British troops worked their way along the rooftops in order to assault the barricade near Langan's pub [7]. Explosions rocked the structure as grenades rained down on the building. The Volunteers returned fire on their attackers, and only a short distance separated the attackers from the defenders. The Volunteers at Reilly's Fort [21] and Monk's Bakery [19] opened fire, pinning the attackers down on the roof. Exposed and without proper cover, the military were forced to withdraw. There was no respite for either side.

Colonel Taylor realised that the street was heavily defended, and decided to employ the use of the armoured personnel carriers in an aggressive counter-attack. The Irish Volunteers watched from their positions as two Armoured Personnel Carriers (APCs) hurtled onto North King Street. Blocked by the barricade, they were only able to travel as far as number 27. The vehicles ground to a halt, disgorging their cargo of soldiers. They proceeded to fire into every house, forcing the occupants to lie down on the floor as bullets tore into the walls above them. Under the cover of the vehicles, 'A' Company began to force entry into the houses. The South Staffs kicked in the doors, or broke them open using sledgehammers. One soldier accidentally discharged his weapon as he attempted to break in a door with his rifle butt, killing Private J.H. Sherwood behind him. The Volunteers opened a rapid fire at the vehicles in an attempt to stop the British from gaining a foothold on the street. Once inside, the South Staffs ran up the stairs and took up firing positions at windows that commanded a view of the barricade at Langan's. The APCs pulled away to reload.

Firing broke out at point-blank range as British soldiers and Irish Volunteers fought a bitter and merciless battle across the narrow roadway. The defenders at Langan's fought desperately to repel attack after attack. Many British troops were wounded as they attempted to storm the barricade. Grenades exploded with brilliant flashes, showering the defenders with splinters and shrapnel. As the APC returned to the Technical School [9] to reload, it was discovered that the driver and his assistant had fainted from wounds they had received. They were quickly replaced, and the vehicle was once again loaded with troops. The carrier then moved off through the smoke of battle.[2]

In an attempt to outflank the Volunteer defences on North King Street, Crown forces manoeuvred out from the back of Ball's Chemist's shop near the smouldering Linenhall Barracks [6]. Volunteer Séan O'Duffy spotted the British troops and shouted to his comrades to 'stand to'. The section in Moore's Coach Factory made ready. Volunteer Peader Breslin took aim and shot dead the first British soldier who moved out from cover.[3] The other Volunteers followed suit, and a barrage of fire was unleashed against the British. The sound of rifle fire was loud and continuous as it reverberated around the building.

Commandant Daly arrived at the Four Courts [3] complex. The building was heavily fortified, and resisting any form of attack from the south side of the River Liffey. He ordered the transfer of some Volunteers to reinforce the posts in and around North King Street. The Commandant was convinced that the British were making a combined effort to obtain a foothold in the area, with a view to an all-out attack. Volunteers grabbed their equipment and moved out. Daly followed them, a service rifle slung over his shoulder.

That evening, the British military decided to launch an attack from the Smithfield area on the west side of the Four Courts. Major Raynor, commanding a detachment of the Sherwood Foresters, was ordered to secure the western approach to the Four Courts so that a British force could be established in the area with a view to launching an all out assault. Colonel Meldon of the 4th Royal Dublin Fusiliers had established his headquarters at the Broadstone Railway Station [12]. Combined forces of the two regiments would secure the area and the 2/5th South

Staffordshire regiment would then attempt to link up the cordon with the 2/6th South Staffs advancing from North King Street.[4] The 2/5th South Staffordshire regiment supported by the 2/7th Sherwood Foresters arrived in Smithfield via a number of armoured cars. The soldiers took up position, and erected a defensive barricade from Queen Street to George's Lane. Under the cover of darkness, they began their advance towards Church Street. The British sustained a number of casualties as they attempted to clear and secure the area of operation. Several times, fire was exchanged with shadowy groups that swerved away into the darkness. For every house secured there were dozens more with potential Volunteers. A muzzle-flash in a window would stop the advance. When the building was stormed, it was often found to be empty except for a few shell casings on the floor. Progress was slow, and Crown forces occupied Egan's Public House at the corner of Smithfield Market, and held this line down to the River Liffey.

British casualties were removed by stretcher-bearers throughout the battle. They were piled into the armoured personnel carriers and taken to the Red Cross station in Dublin Castle. A nurse recalls the dreadful scenes at the castle's casualty-clearing station.

I never thought I would have seen such suffering in the ward that night; the groaning was indescribable. There was a boy in the South Staffords, with the blue face one dreaded to see. Normally he must have been unusually good-looking, and he was not then eighteen. Every few minutes he would sit bolt upright, stripped to the waist, and stare wildly round with unseeing eyes; and when we tried to make him lie down again, would shrink from being touched, and grunt his disapproval. I came into the ward just in time to see screens being put round a bed – it was the first time I had ever seen the face of a dead man.[5]

At the Father Matthew Hall [5], the scene was similar. Volunteer casualties poured into the Red Cross station, many suffering from gunshot wounds or shrapnel injuries. Those that were considered flesh wounds were assisted by the Cumann na mBan, who dressed their wounds.

The Volunteers had no trained doctors in their ranks, and the seriously injured had to be removed under fire to the Richmond Hospital [15]. The stretcher-bearers ran the gauntlet of fire up Church Street, across North King Street, into Brunswick Street and through the gates of the hospital.

As the sound of battle intensified, and the Father Matthew Hall became congested with wounded, Commandant Daly decided to move his command post to the Four Courts. Under continuous sniper fire, Vice-Commandant Piaras Béaslaí and Volunteer Eamon Morkan hauled boxes of ammunition and grenades from the hall to the courts. This involved a number of hazardous journeys crossing barricades while heavily laden with boxes of stores and explosives. The 24 Dublin Metropolitan Police officers who had been taken prisoner on Wednesday were released near the Richmond Hospital. They were very grateful. Daly addressed them, saying, 'Forget all you have seen,' and this was with a chorus of agreement. Many of them thought they were going to be shot and were surprised to have been released.[6]

The firing had become so heavy that Daly decided to remove for safety the Army Pay Corp prisoners held in the Father Matthew Hall. They were escorted to the Bridewell Police Station [29] where they were held under guard. Some time later, a large watermain burst, which flooded the cells on the lower level, threatening to drown the prisoners. The Volunteers managed to stem the flow of water and the prisoners were safely secured for the night.

In the North Dublin Union [14], Father Aloysius O.F.M. attended to the remains of two young boys who had been killed by military snipers. The young boys had gone to the top of the clock tower to see the fires in the city centre, and both were shot dead.

By evening, the glare from the fire had died down and the streets were in semi-darkness. Though it was difficult to see any of the enemy, the Volunteers could hear the sound of boots on the cobbles amongst the din of the rifle fire. Volunteer Patrick Kelly wrote,

I was watching from a window, and noticed a shadow moving near a tenement house about thirty yards from me. I challenged, and a man answered 'friend.' I told him to advance, but he would not do so. While I was calling to him, Lieutenant O'Callaghan shouted from another position, 'shoot him.' On hearing this, the man shouted back in a cockney accent, 'fire away, you will want them all tomorrow.' I fired, and he fell with a loud groan and was pulled into the tenement.[7]

The only guide to a possible target was the flash of a rifle. A scream or groan announced when a bullet had found its target.

EDWARD O'DALY,

Commandaut, 1st Dublin Batt., Irish Republican Army.

Executed May 4th, 1916.

Above: Commandant Edward Daly (not 'O'Daly' as in the image above). Daly commanded the Volunteer forces that occupied the Four Courts and the surrounding areas on Easter Monday 1916. He was executed by the British for his part in the Rising. (Kilmainham Gaol)

The Four Courts.

Photos by Keogh Bros. and T. W. Murphy.

Above: Four Courts. The centre of British justice in Ireland, the Four Courts were completed in 1802. Unlike many other buildings in the city centre, they were largely undamaged by the heavy artillery barrages fired by British guns during the Rising. During the Civil War, however, the building was extensively damaged. (Kilmainham Gaol)

Above: The Chancery Street Gate. It was through this gate that the Volunteers entered the Four Courts on Easter Monday 1916. (D9959, Military Archives)

Above: Buildings on North Brunswick Street as they appeared in a series of photographs taken in the 1950s by the Irish Air Corp of areas that saw conflict during the Rising. (Military Archives)

Above: From the same series, this image shows the westernmost point occupied by Volunteers. (Military Archives)

Above: Fianna Éireann Council with brothers Patrick & Gary Holahan standing and sitting on the left side of the picture. (Patrick Holahan)

Above left: Officers of the 1st Battalion of the Irish Volunteers. Jack Shouldice is standing to the right side of the picture. (Chris Shouldice)

Above right: Volunteer Charles S. Bevan. (Kilmainham Gaol)

Above: British Army Lancers on the Quays, 1916. (The Queen's Royal Lancers Regimental Museum)

Above: The Medical Mission where the survivors of the ill-fated Lancer column took refuge on Monday 24 April and held out there, despite the death of their commander, low ammunition and very few supplies, until they were relieved by improvised armoured cars on Thursday 27 April. (Military Archives)

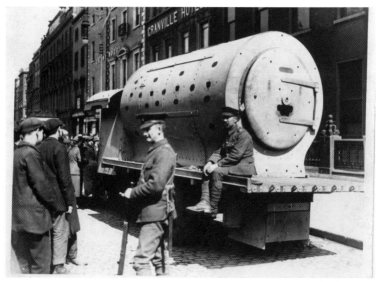

Above: One of the boilers from the Inchicore works converted for use as improvised armoured cars. This one is pictured on Sackville Street near the Granville Hotel. (Mick O'Farrell)

Above left: Clarke's Dairy building as it appeared in the 1950s. This image is from the same series mentioned previously. (Military Archives)

Above right: Seán Heuston, who commanded the Volunteers in the Mendicity Institute. (Kilmainham Gaol)

Above: Lieutenant-Colonel Taylor, Commander of the North Staffordshire Regiment. Front Row, left. (Staffordshire Museum)

Above: Soldiers of the South Staffordshire Regiment manning a checkpoint in Dublin in the aftermath of the 1916 Rising. (Peter Leslie)

Above: Church Street Bridge in the aftermath of the Rising. Note the caption: 'Irish Rebellion, May, 1916. The wreck they made of Church Street. Dublin'. (Daily Sketch)

Above: Survivors of the 1ˢᵗ Battalion of the Irish Volunteers, c. 1950. (Chris Shouldice)

Every now and then a very light shot upwards with a muffled crack and then a hiss as it slowed in to a dazzling shaky probe of magnesium white or green, casting a ghostly glare over the streetscape. This was followed by a barrage of rifle and machine-gun fire. The shouts of commands, the screaming of the wounded and the continuous noise of battle tortured both sides throughout the night. By midnight, after many hours of combat, Lieutenant-Colonel Taylor's gains were practically nil.

General Sir John Grenfell Maxwell, officer in command of his Majesty's forces in Ireland, issued the following proclamation:

Most rigorous measures will be taken by me to stop the loss of life and damage to property which certain misguided persons are causing by their armed resistance to the law. If necessary, I shall not hesitate to destroy all buildings within any area occupied by rebels, and I warn all persons within the area now surrounded by his Majesty's troops, forthwith to leave such areas under the following conditions: (a) Women and children may leave the area from any of the examining posts, and will be allowed to go away free; (b) men may leave by the same examining posts, and will be allowed to go away free, provided the examining officer is satisfied they have taken no part whatever in the disturbance; (c) all other men who present themselves at the said examining posts must surrender unconditionally, together with any arms and ammunition in their possession.[8]

British soldiers, Irish Volunteers and the citizens of Dublin watched as the second city of the empire burned.

Chapter 10

Saturday 29 April 1916: Morning

After 00.00 hours, it became clear to the small Volunteer unit holding Langan's Public House [7] and covering the barricade on Coleraine Street that they were running short of ammunition. The men realised that by daylight the position would be untenable. To avoid being overrun, it was decided to withdraw from the post and make their way to a more secure position. At 03.00 hours, amidst a hail of gunfire and explosions, the Volunteers ran from the building. It was during this withdrawal that Volunteer John Dwan was shot dead, a bullet through the head. Dwan was 25 years old, and was employed at the railway works in Inchicore. The Volunteers fell back, and reinforced the section in 'Reilly's Fort' [21].

Armoured Personnel Carriers filled with the South Staffs raced forward in order to occupy the now vacant Langan's. The military fired in any and every direction from the vehicles. Having seized a foothold on the street, they were soon reinforced by other companies. Inside, the APCs were crowded and smelt of petrol fumes, sweat and fear. Sergeant Samuel Cooper of the 2/6th South Staffs recalled:

Every bullet clanged and jarred through your head. From a confined space it was impossible to return fire. The vehicle did not guarantee complete safety either. 'I remember we backed up to a pub as bullets rattled madly against "the tank" – and one fellow broke a window and we all poured out. It wasn't until daylight we discovered one fellow had been hit, apparently just as he got out. He was lying dead under a window.'[1]

Lieutenant-Colonel Taylor knew that it was suicide to attempt another frontal assault using the same tactics. He had to get his men nearer the target without exposing them before launching an attack. Taylor decided to employ the same tactics as the Volunteers. At 04.00 hours, an APC trundled onto North King Street, and ground to a halt outside number 172. A section from 'A' Company piled out of the vehicle armed with picks and crowbars. They forced their way into the house, and took up position. The troops were ordered to begin 'mouse-holing': tunnelling from one house to another without exposing themselves in order to keep casualties to a minimum. Squad leaders ordered walls to be broken through, and the men began traversing the terraced houses, bypassing the street barricade, bringing them nearer to their quarry. As Private Jack Lovatt of the South Staffs took up a firing position at a window, he was shot dead. The other soldiers crouched low as bullets flew through the windows.

Volunteer Lieutenant Jack Shouldice stared out from behind the fortified frontage of Reilly's public house [21]. The small garrison made ready as an attack in force was expected. Along the line, magazines were inserted into weapons; rifle bolts slid smoothly shut pushing the top round into the chamber. Men took up their firing positions at the windows.

Taylor ordered a section of 'D' Company to move up the street under the cover of the houses. Moving from room to room and from house to house, the South Staffs were soon in position to launch an attack at dawn against 'Reilly's Fort.'

Though they had moved nearer to the Volunteer positions, they still had a considerable amount of open ground to cover. The order to 'fix bayonets' was given, and the South Staffs made ready. A shrill blast of a whistle announced the assault, and British troops charged towards 'Reilly's Fort.' As they advanced, some took the middle of the road while others came on in small rushes under cover of the houses on either side of the street. As they reached Beresford Street, the Volunteers opened fire. Fusillade after fusillade was fired into the ranks of the attackers. Frontal fire from 'Reilly's Fort' and enfilading fire from the Volunteers positioned in Beresford Street and the Malt House tower [31] decimated the attackers. Soldiers screamed in pain, throwing their hands upwards as they dropped their weapons and collapsed to the ground, many writhing in agony while others lay still. In this assault, 9 South Staffs were killed and many more wounded. Their bodies lay on the roadway opposite Sammon's Repository. The remnants of the section fell back in disarray.

In 'Reilly's Fort', empty cartridge and shell cases littered the floor. Weapons and faces were smeared with burnt cordite. The men were covered in dust, and the smoke from their weapons felt bitter in their throats. Ammunition and food were running dangerously low. There had been several abortive attempts to get supplies on Friday. Lieutenant Maurice Collins, the post commander, asked for two men to volunteer to run the gauntlet to the Father Matthew Hall [5] for supplies of ammunition and grenades. Volunteers Edward Delamere and Patrick O'Flanagan came forward. As the men left the building, they were covered by vigorous rifle-fire. An hour later, they were observed making their way back to the post. Cover fire erupted from the building as the two Volunteers ran towards 'Reilly's Fort'. Edward Delamere was leading, and Patrick O'Flanagan followed closely behind. Both men carried bandoliers of ammunition. As they ran across the road towards the door of 'Reilly's', the street was swept by machine-gun fire. Delamere succeeded in making it through the doorway before the machine-gunner traversed his weapon. Volunteer Patrick Flanagan stumbled as he neared the doorway, a full burst of gunfire killing him outright. His body was dragged through the doorway into cover. Volunteer Patrick Flanagan was 24 years old, and lived on Moore Street. His death left a wife and three children. His brother, Michael Flanagan, was also a member of the garrison in 'Reilly's Fort.'[2]

The enemy fire was intense and concentrated, and the 2/5th South Staffs advancing from Smithfield had reached a position about 30 yards from 'Reilly's Fort.' It was vital that the cordon on North King Street was sealed.

At 09.00 hours on Saturday morning, Lieutenant Maurice Collins called together the section commanders and ordered the evacuation of Reilly's Fort. The section commanders, including Lieutenant Jack Shouldice and his unit, discussed the best way to leave the building. They opened the front door, but it was immediately apparent that the enemy had the main street covered. Any movement immediately attracted a rip of bullets that showered the outside of the building. It was decided to evacuate the building as a group. The men were ordered to line up on the ground floor of the building and make ready. The front door was opened, but Lieutenant Collins stated that when he gave the order to 'charge' in a sufficiently loud voice it was to be ignored. Lieutenant Shouldice was then to shout a second order to charge, and the men were to jump from a window into the street and run towards the barricade on Church Street. This action would confuse the military who were within earshot of the building and covering the front door. The first order was shouted, and the men made ready to move out. Lieutenant Shouldice shouted the second order and the Volunteers, one by one, jumped through the window and rushed out across the fire-swept zone towards Church Street. In seconds, the garrison were in the open and racing for cover. A machine-gun burst hit the heel of a boot of one man, and he collapsed in the roadway. Lying still, he feigned death for a few moments until the firing ceased. He then jumped up and continued across the roadway and into cover. In all, about 14 Volunteers, the entire remaining garrison, made it safely from 'Reilly's.'[3] The Volunteers manning the barricade in Church Street covered the retreat by opening fire on any attempt of the British to move out from their positions.

By 11.00 hours on Saturday 29 April, 'D' Company of the 2/6th South Staffs held the lower part of North King Street, driving a wedge between the Volunteer positions. A number of British soldiers rushed forward and occupied the now vacant 'Reilly's Fort.'

However, the soldiers soon realised they had made a mistake. The Volunteers manning the barricades on Church Street and on Beresford Street opened fire on 'Reilly's Fort.' A number of soldiers made an attempt to leave 'Reilly's Fort', but were shot down. The remainder found themselves surrounded and cut off from their main force.

Chapter 11

Saturday 29 April 1916: Afternoon

At around 13.00 hours, Colonel Taylor launched an attack against the barricade at North Brunswick Street. British soldiers rushed forward and were met by a hail of fire. They fell back in disarray, unable to relieve the British unit now cut off in 'Reilly's Fort' [21].

Gary and Patrick Holohan rallied their men and counter-attacked in an attempt to push the British out of 'Reilly's' and back down North King Street. Laying down a covering fire, a small party advanced through the rear of Monk's Bakery [19], and then worked their way around into Neary's shop on North King Street. Entering through the rear door, the men took up their positions. On the other side of 'Reilly's Fort', the Volunteers approached the building through Ball's Drug Store. A group of the South Staffs had occupied Kavanagh's shop on North King Street. With only a few yards separating the two sides, gunfire erupted at close quarters as each side desperately tried to kill the other.

A section from 'D' Company, South Staffs, moved forward and reached the junction of Church Street and North King Street. They rushed the barricade at upper Church Street, forcing the Volunteers to retire back to the barricade at Mary's Lane. Volunteer Lieutenant Joe McGuinness rallied the Volunteers and counter-attacked the British force. Leading a charge down Church Street, the Lieutenant managed to regain the barricade outside the Father Matthew Hall. During this action, Volunteer Seán Hurley was shot in the head and killed. He was 29 years old, and was a member of 'F' Company, 1st Battalion. Also at this position, Volunteer Seán Bernard Howard was fatally wounded. He was 39 years old, and lived at Temple Cottages in Broadstone.

One of the Franciscan Capuchin Fathers – whose church was fated to be the centre of the battleground – was on duty during the week in the Richmond Hospital [15] when a Volunteer Red Cross bearer brought word that Seán Bernard Howard had been brought to the Father Matthew Hall dangerously wounded, and that it was necessary that he should immediately be brought to hospital. This priest, and Dr D. Flanagan, immediately volunteered to take the wounded man to hospital. In going to the hall, they had to cross North King Street, then swept by a terrific crossfire from both ends. On reaching the street, they stood for a moment to breathe a short prayer and then quietly walked across. Although the bullets whistled around them, they reached the opposite side in safety. In the hall, a large Red Cross flag was thrown over the priest's shoulder and, thus enveloped, he and the doctor made the return journey to hospital in safety bearing the wounded man on the stretcher. Howard died later that evening.[1]

***

The 2/6th South Staffs were now in a position to link up with the 2/5th South Staffords that were pressing forward from Smithfield. As 16.00 hours approached, the Volunteers positioned in Clarke's Dairy [20] and Monk's Bakery [19] noticed that the British soldiers were successfully sealing the cordon on North King Street.

Reinforcing their position at Moore's Coach House [18], the Volunteers made ready for an assault on their post. They realised that they were in danger of being cut off, and sent out a party of four men to reconnoitre the area to see if it would be possible to break through the British cordon and link up with the main body of Irish Volunteers on Church Street. As the Recon unit moved out, Volunteer section commander Philip Walsh was shot dead. Walsh was 27 years old, and resided in Manor Place, Dublin.

British forces moving westwards and eastwards on North King Street had linked up and reinforced the garrison in 'Reilly's Fort.' A wedge had been driven between Daly's forces, isolating those Volunteer posts to the north of North King Street. British troops immediately took up firing positions in the windows facing the Volunteer positions. An order was given to 'open fire.'

A barrage of rifle-fire erupted from the building towards Moore's Coach Factory. Volunteers Peter Paul Manning and Patrick Farrell, in position on the top floor, were shot dead.

A member of 'G' Company, Manning was 25 years old and lived on Broadstone Avenue in Dublin. He was employed as a machine ruler, and was the sole support of his widowed mother. Farrell was 19 years old. He was employed as a plasterer. A doctor and a priest were sent for, and soon arrived, despite the heavy fire in the area. A Red Cross flag was displayed from the window of the building in order to assure safe passage for the priest and the doctor, but was riddled with bullets within a few minutes.

From 15.00 hours until 19.30 hours, the Volunteers on North Brunswick Street made a determined effort to hold the last contested position. After almost five hours of continuous combat, the unit in North Brunswick Street prepared to fall back. Assisting their wounded, they pulled out and made their way towards Clarke's and Moore's. Outgunned and outnumbered, Volunteer Sergeant Seán O'Connor ordered the Volunteer unit to fall back. At 19.30 hours, they moved out and joined the rest of the battalion at the Four Courts [3]. As they moved down Bow Street and turned left at Hammond Lane, a number of shots rang out hitting and wounding three men in their feet. The Volunteers dragged their wounded comrades into cover. They crawled back to the Four Courts, constantly being sniped at but without further casualties.[2]

At 20.00 hours, Commandant Daly ordered all men manning barricades to fall back to the Four Courts. Volunteer Eamon Tierney sought permission from Captain Fionan Lynch to retrieve the tricolour flag that still flew from the lance that the Volunteers had placed in the manhole at the Junction of Church Street and North King Street. Tierney rushed forward through a hail of gunfire, took the flag from the lance and returned back safely. As the Volunteers withdrew from their posts, Company Commander Frank Fahy was found lying in the roadway. Many thought he was wounded, but in fact he had suffered from a heart attack. A number of Volunteers carried the officer through the gate and handed him over to the care of the Cumann na mBan.

At 16.00 hours, the situation at the Red Cross Hospital in the Father Matthew Hall [5] had greatly deteriorated. Medical supplies were running low, and wounded Volunteers lay on the bloodstained floor. In order to prevent further suffering of the injured it was decided to send a Volunteer Red Cross officer to the British military to ask for a possible evacuation of the wounded. After some time the Volunteer returned with the verbal answer, 'You are all rebels and outlaws and you will get none of the amenities of war.'[3]

At Clarke's and Moore's, the Volunteers under the command of Paddy Holohan prepared their positions for a full assault from the South Staffs. Surrounded, the Volunteers prepared to make a last stand. Using an axe, the Volunteers worked desperately to break through the walls into houses on either side of their post to give themselves a better field of fire. Three holes were bored in the wall that commanded the approach from North Brunswick Street. Broken bricks and plaster were loaded into pillow covers and placed on the window-sills. The British attack was announced as machine-gun fire raked the front of the buildings. The smashed masonry produced huge clouds of dust, from which British soldiers emerged running as if through a wall of smoke. A Canadian soldier, on leave from France, launched the attack. Carrying a satchel of hand grenades, the soldier jumped the barricade, but, before he could extract the pin from a bomb, he was killed in a barrage of rifle fire. As the military advanced, the Volunteers discarded their rifles and opened fire with revolvers and automatic pistols. The British fell back, taking their wounded with them. There was a slight lull in the fighting as the British attempted to move closer without exposing themselves. At the blast of a whistle, they charged forward again into a hail of gunfire. Another British soldier was shot and seriously wounded in full view of the Volunteer positions. Holohan shouted, 'take in that man, we won't fire.' A sergeant in the South Staffs cursed the Volunteers and refused to take in the wounded man. A while later, there was an impromptu ceasefire as the wounded soldier was carried off the roadway. The sergeant moved forward, took cover behind a street-light standard and shouted instructions to his men. Exposing himself to take a shot, the sergeant leaned forward and was immediately shot and badly wounded. Another impromptu ceasefire enabled British soldiers to carry the wounded sergeant off the street.[4]

Monk's Bakery [19] was under accurate sniper fire, and Volunteer Larry Lawlor, a member of 'A' Company, was seriously wounded. The sniper was located in a house at the corner of Church Street. The sniper was not firing from the lower part of the window, but had lowered the top frame about four inches, and standing on a piece of furniture was firing from the top left-hand corner. Volunteer Patrick Kelly took careful aim at the British sniper and opened fire. He watched as the man's body fell to the floor.[5]

Shootouts were common as the Volunteers picked off British soldiers who had taken up sniper positions. The Volunteers had not eaten since morning, and ammunition was running low. The smell of cordite and the hot, oily smell of their rifles filled the rooms. Holohan moved from post to post encouraging his small garrison of less than sixty men. Surrounded and cut off, he knew there was no hope of relief. It was to be a fight to the death.[6]

Chapter 12

Saturday 29 April 1916:
Evening

At 18.00 hours, Nurse Elizabeth O' Farrell and Revd Father Columbus O.S.F.C. conveyed the surrender order from Patrick Pearse, Commander-in-Chief of the Irish Volunteers, to Commandant Daly at the Four Courts [3]. Bearing a small white flag, the two made their way through the British lines towards the courts. Nurse O'Farrell wrote:

> We passed Charles Street, and went over into the side entrance of the Four Courts. We called in for some Volunteers and saw Captain.... We told him we had a message for Commandant Daly. He told us we would have to go round to the quays to the corner of Church Street; this we did and found Commandant Daly strongly entrenched there. I gave him the order, and told him of the headquarters' surrender. He was very much cut up

about it but accepted his orders, as a soldier should. He walked back with us to the side entrance, and by this time the news had got about of the surrender, and several officers of the Republican Army were down at the rails waiting for us.[1]

Daly addressed his officers, stating that an order to surrender had been received from Pearse. Many of the officers were shocked at the decision, and Piaras Béaslaí stated what most of the others thought: that the Four Courts position was impregnable and could be held for a month. The Volunteers had not considered surrender at any level. However, Daly ordered that all men should obey their Commander-in-Chief's order and lay down their arms. As they downed their weapons and assembled outside, a British Major queried the number of Volunteers who had surrendered. He said, 'If I had known that this was the extent of the garrison here, you would have been out of this by half past twelve on Monday morning last.'[2] After surrendering their arms, the Four Courts garrison, and those who had withdrawn from the outlying posts, was formed into fours, and the battalion, headed by Commandant Edward Daly, Vice-Commandant Piaras Béaslaí and Captain Eamon Duggan, marched out of the Four Courts by way of the Chancery Gate to the quayside. They were marched by way of the quays, Capel Street and Parnell Street until they reached the Rotunda, where the officers were taken from the column. The remainder were marched to the Parnell monument on Sackville Street.

Piaras Béaslaí wrote, 'a British officer approached the group and asked, "who is in charge of these men?" Commandant Daly proudly replied, "I am. At all events, I was." A remark which, he must have known, signed his death-warrant.'[3]

The Cumann na mBan detachment that were caring for the wounded in the courts were permitted to remain overnight in the building. It was arranged that the wounded and nursing staff be removed the following morning in ambulances.

***

But the fighting wasn't over. While their comrades in the Four Courts [3] were surrendering, the volunteers in Clarke's Dairy [20], led by Volunteer Garry Holohan, prepared to launch another assault on the British in North King Street. The men loaded their weapons and primed their grenades. As they made ready to move out, Revd Father Albert O.F.S.C., Dr Miles and Dr O'Carroll arrived at Clarke's Dairy, and informed Volunteer officer Patrick Holohan of the surrender. The young officer stated that he had heard nothing of the surrender, and informed the men that his section had decided on a fight to the finish.[4]

As the peace envoys left the building, firing once again commenced. Father Augustine and Father Aloysius asked for a meeting with the British officer in command. Accompanied by a Red Cross officer, the three men arrived at the Blanchardstown Mill, then occupied by the military. Lieutenant-Colonel Taylor, the British commander in the area, arrived and discussed a possible ceasefire with the Volunteers. It was decided to send the Red Cross officer to parley with the Volunteer officer in command. As they were about to leave, a number of shots rang out, almost hitting Lieutenant-Colonel Taylor. The British officer drew his revolver and covered the Red Cross officer, believing that it may be a ploy to get him killed. Father Augustine stepped forward and volunteered to go himself. As he walked towards North Brunswick Street, the firing ceased.

Volunteer Patrick Holohan, officer commanding, stated that he would not make any terms with the British military. However, if Father Augustine thought it was necessary, the young officer would agree to a temporary truce in order to remove the wounded. An official truce between British and Irish forces was brokered from 19.30 hours on Saturday evening until 10.00 hours on Sunday morning. The British soldiers stationed in the Broadstone Railway Station [12] were notified of the cease-fire by Dr O'Carroll of the Richmond Hospital [15]. A military sergeant and a corporal accompanied him. An unarmed Volunteer accompanied the party, while another Volunteer was held as a 'hostage' until the party's safe return.

Gary Holohan's unit were told to stand down. During the cease-fire, two British officers advanced a short distance beyond the demarcation line agreed upon. They were warned by the Volunteer sentry to halt and return to their own side. They ignored this challenge until the Volunteers at Clarke's Dairy turned out an armed guard, forcing the two officers to return to their own side.

Towards nightfall, the lull in the fighting provided an opportunity for the Volunteers to evacuate some of their wounded. Though the main body of Volunteers had surrendered at the Four Courts, a group of Cumann na mBan remained with the wounded in the Father Matthew Hall [5]. It was decided to remove the seriously wounded to the Richmond Hospital. This was arranged by Michael O'Foghludha. Some of the slightly wounded managed to escape to safe houses in the area. The

Cumann na mBan, assisted by a number of medical students from the hospital, carried the wounded on stretchers from the Father Matthew Hall to the Richmond Hospital. Labouring throughout the night, the group avoided the military pickets on North King Street and safely evacuated all the wounded.

Having completed their duty, they returned to the now deserted Father Matthew Hall. There were four staff remaining: the Elliott sisters, Kathleen Kenny and Eilis Ui Chonaill. The women spent the night in the church in a room beside the high altar. They slept and waited anxiously for the dawn.

Chapter 13

Sunday 30 April 1916

Early on Sunday morning, an official copy of the order for surrender signed by Patrick Pearse was conveyed to the young Volunteer, Patrick Holohan. He consulted with his men in relation to this order. He ordered his men to move out from their positions and assemble in the street. Under the watchful eye of the British Crown Forces, Holohan called his men to attention. He addressed his men with the following words:

Fellow soldiers of the Irish Republican Army. I have just received a communication from Commandant Pearse calling on us to surrender, and you will agree with me that this is the hardest task we have been called upon to perform during this eventful week, but we came into this fight for Irish independence in obedience to the commands of our higher officers and now in obedience to their wishes we must surrender. I know you would, like myself, prefer to be with our comrades who have already fallen in the fight – we, too, should rather die in this glorious struggle then submit to the enemy. The treatment you may expect in the future you may judge from the past.[1]

Holohan's troop consisted of 58 Volunteers. They were marched under guard to Dublin Castle. Once there, they were lined up against the main wall of the castle and rigorously searched and interrogated by detectives. They were then transferred to Richmond Barracks in Inchicore.

The four members of the Cumann na mBan who had taken refuge in the church now planned their escape. It was devised that at Mass on Sunday morning the women would escape by mingling with the crowd. Standing in the church during the service, the women noticed that there were many Volunteers in the congregation planning to escape in a similar fashion.

When we came out of the church there were crowds outside, people who had come in search of their dear ones or to make enquiries about them. This was a great help to us in moving off. We made our way for home, back through the narrow streets. Every street corner was now lined with British Tommies, and after zigzagging from one street to another in order to avoid the soldiers, we reached North Frederick Street in the evening, having passed another day without food.[2]

Those who surrendered had spent the night in the grounds of the Rotunda hospital and at the Parnell Monument in Sackville Street. Though the Volunteers had been defeated in battle, their spirits remained high. This angered many of the British troops guarding the prisoners. A Captain Percival Lea-Wilson of the 5th Battalion of the Royal Irish Regiment singled out Thomas Clarke and Edward Daly. Both men had been searched, and papers and personal belongings were scattered on the ground. A British NCO passing was asked by Daly to allow him to pick up the papers. The NCO handed the items back to Daly.

When Lea-Wilson discovered this action he called the NCO, and berated him for his act of kindness, saying, 'are you a bloody servant for the rebels?' He stripped Thomas Clarke, and made him stand naked on the steps of the Rotunda Hospital in view of the nursing staff. Wilson then shouted, 'That old bastard is Commander-in-Chief. He keeps a tobacco shop across the Street. Nice General for your fucking army.'[3] Over 300 British soldiers, civilians and Irish Volunteer prisoners in particular two young Volunteers, Michael Collins and Liam Tobin, witnessed this act of humiliation.

After this ordeal, the prisoners were marched to Richmond Barracks and kept under guard. Volunteer officers were identified and separated from their men. In the days and weeks that followed, the men of the 1st Battalion were marched to the North Wall and brought to Stafford Prison in England. Here they remained for a number of weeks, before finally being sent to Frongoch camp in Wales. Many of their officers would have a different fate.

Chapter 14

May 1916: Executions

While the fighting was over, not all the shooting was. During a military Court Martial held in secret at Richmond Barracks, Commandant Edward Daly was charged:

> [He] Did an act, to wit did take part in an armed rebellion and in the waging of war against his majesty the King, such act being of such a nature as to be calculated to be prejudicial to the Defence to the Realm, and being done with the intention and for the purpose of assisting the enemy.[1]

After a brief trial, Edward Daly was found guilty and sentenced to death. On the evening of 3 May 1916, he was transferred to Kilmainham Gaol. In the early hours of the following day, he was visited by his sisters, Kathleen, Madge and Laura. After a brief conversation, in which Daly spoke highly of his men, Madge Daly recalled a soldier entering the cell and shouting:

'Time up' and our interview was at an end. We kissed and embraced our boy, once only, and walked from the cell without a tear or moan, our heads up. Looking back now, I wonder how we bore up. But God helped us, and Ned too, with his great courage and heart. The cell door banged behind us, and we walked down the endless stairs. I felt Laura's steps faltering and, fearing she would faint, whispered to her: 'Keep up. You musn't break down here.' She answered, in a whisper too, 'I'll be all right.'[2]

Between 4.00 hours and 4.30 hours on the morning of 4 May 1916, Commandant Edward Daly was executed by firing squad in the Stonebreakers' Yard at Kilmainham Gaol. According to the priest who heard Daly's last confession, the officer faced the firing squad 'calm and brave.'[3] His body was removed from Kilmainham Gaol, and buried in quicklime in the yard of Arbour Hill Prison.

Captain Seán Heuston, the young Fianna Officer who had held the Mendicity Institute [2], also found himself before a Court Martial. Captain A.W. MacDermot of the Royal Dublin Fusiliers stated:

On 26 April, I was present when an assault party of the 10th Royal Dublin Fusiliers took the Mendicity Institute. Twenty-three men surrendered on that occasion. I identify the four prisoners as having been in the body of men surrendered. They left their arms, except their revolvers, in the Mendicity Institute when they surrendered. Some of them still wore revolvers. One officer of the 10th Royal Dublin Fusiliers was killed and nine men wounded by fire from this institute. On 24 April, I searched the building when they surrendered. I found several rifles, and several thousand rounds of ammunition for both revolvers and rifles. I found six or seven bombs, charged and with fuses in them ready for use.

I found the following papers: an order signed by James Connolly, one of the signatories of the Proclamation, directing Captain Heuston to 'Seize the Mendicity at all costs.'[4]

Heuston was also found guilty and sentenced to death.

On Monday 8 May 1916, Father Albert O.F.M. Cap. accompanied the young officer in to the Stonebreakers' Yard of Kilmainham Gaol. He wrote:

A soldier directed Seán and myself to a corner of the yard, a short distance from the outer wall of the prison. Here there was a box, and Seán was told to sit down upon it. He was perfectly calm and said with me for the last time: 'My Jesus mercy.' I had scarcely moved away a few yards when a volley went off, and this noble soldier of Irish freedom fell dead. I rushed over to anoint him; his whole face seemed transformed and lit up with a grandeur and brightness that I had never before noticed....[5]

Heuston was executed between 3.45 hours and 4.05 hours. It is interesting to note that Heuston was not a signatory of the Proclamation, or a member of the military council. It is in all probability that the officer was executed for the havoc and casualties he inflicted on the Royal Dublin Fusiliers as they attempted to advance along the quays. Heuston was 25 years old, and had been employed by the Great Southern and Western Railway Company.

The history of the 2/5th Battalion of the Sherwood Foresters states:

> Every Sinn Féiner who was condemned to death stood in the courtyard at Kilmainham before the firing-squad, drawn from a sister Battalion to our own, steadily, like men, without flinching, and without support. All faced the rifles not as craven rebels, but like men dying for a great idea. Soldiers who were present, ever susceptible to courage whenever they find it, acknowledge this.[6]

In defence of his decision to execute many of those who had participated in the Rising, General Sir John Maxwell wrote to Prime Minister Herbert Asquith:

> In view of the gravity of the rebellion, and its connection with German intrigue and propaganda, and in view of the great loss of life and destruction of property resulting therefrom, the General officer Commanding in Chief, Irish Command, has found it imperative to inflict the most severe sentence to the known organisers of this detestable Rising, and on those Commanders who took an active part in the actual fighting which occurred. It is hoped that these examples will be sufficient to act as a deterrent to intrigues and to bring home to them that the murder of his Majesty's subjects or other acts calculated to imperil the safety of the realm will not be tolerated.[7]

In total, 97 men were condemned to death for their part in the 1916 Rising. Twelve were executed at Kilmainham Gaol, one in Cork and one in London. Popular opinion in Ireland as well as England put pressure on the government to stop the executions. The remaining prisoners were sentenced to penal servitude, and were transported to prisons in England, and later interned in Frongoch prison camp in Wales.

Chapter 15

Bloody Murder

As the smoke and dust of battle settled on North King Street, a gruesome discovery was unearthed in the basement of number 177, a licensed premises belonging to Mrs Mary O'Rourke. Acting on information received, Mr A. Moynihan, borough surveyor, searched the cellar, and discovered that a portion of the floor was softer than the surrounding area. Dr Mathew Russell, Assistant Medical Officer of Health for the Dublin area, was called, and he instructed council sanitary staff to excavate the ground. About 12 inches from the surface they discovered the body of a male. Underneath this body, they discovered another body of a man. Both were fully dressed. On investigating the cellar, they found that the excess soil from the shallow grave had been deposited under the slide where the barrels were lowered from the street above. The bodies were identified as those of Patrick Bealen and James Healy, both of whom had disappeared during the fighting on North King Street. The bodies were exhumed and taken to the city morgue.

This discovery prompted an official investigation. On Friday 12 May 1916, at the opening of an inquest into the suspicious deaths of the men, allegations of misconduct were levelled against the military authorities on service in North King Street. The coroner adjourned the hearing and notified the military authorities in order that they may be represented in the court.

This, however, was just the beginning. In the days that followed the cessation of hostilities, a number of statements were taken by the police authorities with regard to civilian deaths in the North King Street area between 18.00 hours on April 28 to 10.00 hours on April 29 1916.

Michael Noonan (34) and George Ennis (51) were killed at number 174 North King Street. Ennis, mortally wounded, pleaded with his wife to find the soldiers so that they may return and finish him off. At number 170, Thomas Hickey (38), Christopher Hickey (16) and Peter Connolly (39) were killed, their bodies showing bayonet marks. At number 172, Michael Hughes (50) and John Walsh (56) were shot dead. Mrs Ellen Walsh stated that on Sunday afternoon she witnessed soldiers playing cards on a rug thrown over her husband's dead body. John Beirnes (50) was killed in Coleraine Street, shot dead from a building known to be occupied by Crown forces. Peter Joseph Lawless (21), James McCarthy (36), James Finnigan (about 40) and Patrick Hoey (25) were all killed at the Louth Dairy at number 27 North King Street. A soldier was overheard to say, 'the little man made a great struggle for his life and tried to throw himself out of the window, but we got him.'[1]

On Tuesday May 16, the hearing resumed. Dr Louis A. Byrne, city coroner, began the inquest into the deaths of Patrick Bealen (30), who had been employed as a foreman at Mrs

O'Rourke's licensed house at 177 North King Street, and James Healy (44), who was employed at Messrs Jameson's Distillery [8], Bow Street.

Major Rhodes, Assistant Provost Marshal, 59th Division, and Captain R.M. Sheppard of the Staffordshire regiment represented the military authorities. Inspector Travers represented the police and Mr J.C.R. Lardner appeared on behalf of the deceased under instruction from Mr John J. McDonald.

Mrs Mary O' Rourke, the proprietress of number 177 North King Street, under examination from Mr Lardner, stated that the military entered her premises at 00.00 hours on 28 April.[2] She had taken refuge in the cellar with her three children, her cook and Patrick Bealen. They were there a number of hours before the military arrived. A sergeant accompanied by a private searched the women's 13-year-old son and Bealen. Everyone was then removed from the cellar to the kitchen of the house that was located on the second floor. Initially, two soldiers stood guard, who were then later joined by a third. Before daybreak, Bealen was removed from the kitchen by some of the soldiers. Early on Saturday morning, an officer arrived and instructed that the remaining people be removed to a larger room as the kitchen was too small.

Dr Meldon, who examined the bodies, gave evidence that in his opinion the shots that killed the men had been fired from a considerable distance. The motive of robbery was dismissed as Michael Brophy, attendant in the Coroner's Court, said he found £7 in notes and gold tied via a shoelace to the back of Bealen's shirt.

Mrs Roseánna Knowles of 23 Lurgan Street [30] was called to give evidence. Living in close proximity to North King Street, a number of soldiers were billeted in her house during the week of hostilities. In conversation with the soldiers, she asked if there were many casualties. They replied that there were many killed on both sides. One soldier said that he pitied the poor fellow at the corner (O' Rourke's). 'I pitied him from my heart, though I had to shoot him. He made me tea.' The soldier recalled that the prisoner was ushered down in to the cellar in O'Rourke's. At gunpoint the prisoner gave the soldiers his ring and his penknife. The military hadn't the heart to shoot him straight, and they told him to go back up the stairs. As he began to ascend the stairs, the soldiers opened fire, killing Patrick Bealen. The soldier produced the penknife but said he had lost the ring.[3]

In defence, Major Rhodes submitted the following statement by Lieutenant-Colonel H. Taylor, commander of the 2/6th South Staffordshire regiment, that was read aloud in court by the coroner.

I cannot discover any military witnesses as to the manner in which the two men, Patrick Bealen and James Healy, met with their deaths, but I cannot believe the allegations made at the inquest can be correct. Patrick Bealen was certainly never brought to the guardroom. To the best of my knowledge and belief, during the military operation in Capel Street and King Street, which lasted from 6 a.m. on Friday, 28 April, until the truce was declared on the afternoon of Saturday 29 (and which were, in fact, continued for some hours after that by the rebels in that area), only those houses were entered by the military which the exigencies of the cases rendered actually necessary, and no persons were attacked by the troops other than those who were assisting the rebels, and found with arms in their possession.

The premises No. 177 North King Street were indicated to me as one of the houses from which the troops had been repeatedly fired upon, and the troops were also continually fired upon both during the night of 26 April, and the whole of the following day, from the distillery, at which the deceased man, James Healy, was stated to have been employed. The operations in the portion of King Street between Linenhall Street and Church Street were conducted under circumstances of greatest difficulty and danger for the troops engaged, who were subjected to severe fire, not only from behind several barricades, which had been constructed across King Street, and other barricades in Church Street and the side streets, but also from practically every house in the portion of King Street and other buildings overlooking it.

Strong evidence of these difficulties and dangers afforded by the fact it took the troops from 10.00 a.m. on 28 April until 2 p.m. on 29 to force their way along King Street from Linenhall Street to Church Street, a distance of 150 yards only; and that the casualties sustained by the regiment (the great majority of which occurred at this spot) numbered five officers (including two captains) wounded, 14 NCOs and men killed and 28 wounded.

I may add (1) that the rebels for some hours after the truce was declared continued firing on my men, who, although they sustained several further casualties, did not reply; and (2) that during these continued hostilities after the truce the rebels, by firing on the R.A.M.C. (one of whom was wounded) prevented the removal of some of the wounded for several hours, and the latter could only be ultimately removed by means of an armoured car.

I am satisfied that during these operations the troops
under my command showed great moderation and restraint
under exceptionally difficult and trying circumstances.[4]

The verdict the jury returned stated that Patrick Bealen and
James Healy died from shock and haemorrhage that resulted
from bullet wounds inflicted by a soldier or soldiers in whose
custody they were unarmed and unoffending prisoners. The jury
dismissed the explanation given by the military authorities as
being unsatisfactory.

In order to appease the local populace, the military held an
identity parade at Straffan in County Kildare in order to offer
the witnesses the opportunity to identify those involved. Lieutenant-Colonel Taylor certified that every man in his battalion
was seen by the witnesses. However, the witnesses failed to identify any of the soldiers. Though almost 2,000 troops were
paraded, it was soon discovered that several members of the
battalion had already been transferred back to England. Official
papers reveal that one particular soldier came to the attention
of General Sir John Maxwell in relation to the North King
Street deaths. Corporal W. Bullock of the 2/6th South Staffordshire regiment was named as a possible suspect. In defence of
the soldier's actions, General Maxwell made the following statement to a journalist of the *Daily Mail*:

Possibly unfortunate incidents, which we should regret
now, may have occurred. It did not, perhaps, always follow
that where shots were fired from a particular house the
inmates were always necessarily aware of it or guilty, but
how were the soldiers to discriminate? They saw their

comrades killed beside them by hidden and treacherous assailants, and it is even possible that under the horrors of this peculiar attack some of them 'saw red.'[5]

No members of the 2/6th South Staffordshire regiment were ever charged with the unlawful killing of Patrick Bealen, James Healy or any of the other civilians on North King Street. Bullock survived the Great War and disappeared into obscurity.

To this day, the case of the deaths in North King Street remains unsolved.

Chapter 16

Aftermath

The centre of Dublin city, the second city of the British Empire, had been virtually destroyed. The smouldering ruin and skeletal buildings were evidence of the battles that had been fought during Easter week of 1916. British regiments remained on standby as martial law was declared throughout the country. Detachments of troops were sent to all four provinces in order to detain suspects and search for weapons. The heavy-handed approach by the military caused resentment amongst the citizens of Ireland. The South Staffordshire regiment remained in Dublin until mid-May, and then moved out to Straffan in County Kildare. They received over 100 replacements for the men killed and wounded during the Rising. In July, the Battalion moved to the Phoenix Park in Dublin and rejoined the other Battalions of the 176th Brigade. In February 1917, the Battalion moved to the killing fields of the Western front.

No special list of honours was issued in connection with the services rendered by the military during the 1916 Rising. Captain J.S. Sheppard and acting Corporal J.S. Barrett of the South Staffordshire regiment were both mentioned in despatches for distinguished services in connection with the rebellion. General Sir John Maxwell wrote:

Many incidents of very gallant behaviour have been brought to my notice, which I am unable to refer to in this order, but I must express my admiration for the conduct of a small detachment from the 6th Reserve Cavalry Regiment, which, when conveying ammunition was attacked in Charles Street, and after a splendid defence for three and a half days, during which their leaders were struck down, safely delivered the ammunition.[1]

The wounded Volunteers who had been evacuated to the Richmond Hospital [15] evaded capture by the British military. Sir Thomas Myles, the doctor in charge, protected the Volunteers from any interference by the police or military authorities. The delay caused by the medical staff enabled many of the men to escape capture and internment.[2]

Colonel Henry Thomas Ward Allatt, the officer who devised the idea of the Armoured Personnel Carriers, was wounded near the South Dublin Union and died on 8 May 1916. A retired officer, he had been re-employed as a recruitment officer at the outbreak of World War One. He was buried at Aldershot Military Cemetery, Hampshire, and was posthumously mentioned in despatches.

With the failure of the Easter Rising, the Irish Volunteer command structure was virtually wiped out. The majority of militant republicans found themselves imprisoned in mainland Britain. By June 1917, however, most of these prisoners had been released and returned to a country still bearing the scars of the rebellion. A new force, the Irish Republican Army, with new commanders, was established and many of those who fought in 1916 joined its ranks. During the Irish war for Independence, Peader Clancy, the young officer who had held the Church Street Bridge [1] barricade, was killed along with Dick McKee in what the British authorities described as an attempted escape from Dublin Castle on 20 November 1920. It is alleged that both men were tortured and killed after they refused to give information.

On 15 June 1920, four years after the Easter Rising of 1916, Captain Percival Lea-Wilson, the officer who had humiliated Thomas Clarke and Edward Daly outside the Rotunda Hospital, but who was by then a District Inspector in the Royal Irish Constabulary, was shot and killed. It was 9.45 hours, and he had just purchased a morning newspaper and was making his way home to his house in Gorey, County Wexford. Newspapers reported that 'the police officer's body had been riddled with bullets.' His death was allegedly in retribution for the ill treatment of Thomas Clarke, and had been planned by Michael Collins and Liam Tobin, by then senior members of the Irish Republican Army.[3] An interesting footnote to this story is that his wife, Marie Lea-Wilson, donated the Caravaggio painting, *The Taking of Christ* to the Jesuits in 1934 in gratitude for the support she received from them on the death of her husband. The painting is now on permanent loan to the National Gallery of Ireland.

In the aftermath of the 1916 Rising, the struggle for Irish Independence continued. Brothers Frank and Jack Shouldice, as well as Patrick and Gary Holohan, continued fighting against Crown forces in Ireland. Evading army and police patrols, these men fought alongside Michael Collins and Eamon De Valera for an independent republic.

Chapter 17

April 1916:
Military Success and
Military Failure

Derived from the Greek word *Strategos*, military strategy deals with the planning and conduct of campaigns, the movement and disposition of forces and the deception of the enemy. Carl Von Clausewitz, the father of modern strategic studies, defines military strategy as 'the employment of battles to gain the end of war.'[1]

In 1916, the position of Commandant Edward Daly's 1st Battalion in the Four Courts [3] and their positions on North King Street were of great military importance. As a commander, Daly sought to apply the forces at his disposal in a decisive way. His defence of this built-up area was organised around key terrain features, buildings, and areas that preserved the integrity of the defence and that afforded the defender ease of movement. Daly organised and planned his defence by

considering obstacles, avenues of approach, key terrain, observation of fields of fire, cover and concealment, fire hazards and
communication restrictions.[2]

In relation to the tactics used by the Volunteers, the history
of the 2/6th Battalion of the North Staffordshire regiment
states:

> North King Street was strongly held by rebels, and it
> immediately became obvious that anything in the nature
> of a direct frontal attack would be abortive. In such mean
> and compact streets, the barricade system of the rebels
> was indeed formidable. The successful storming of a bar-
> ricade achieved no more then to drive its defenders into
> the houses, and having emerged by the back doors they
> were able to repeat their resistance farther along the street.
> The street was defended by a series of such barricades;
> crude affairs composed largely of household furniture.
> The strength of them consisted in the fact that they rein-
> forced or were reinforced by the sniping-posts in the
> houses on the street. The barricade delayed the troops and
> made them a steady target; the sniping-posts, being con-
> stituted for the most part of isolated riflemen shooting
> from sandbagged windows and not whole houses held in
> force, gave deadly effect to the flimsy barricades. What-
> ever might be the degree of the rebels' valour, there could
> be no criticism of their discretion. In this North King
> Street they had situated themselves as to be able to inflict
> maximum casualties on the English troops with minimum
> loss to themselves.[3]

The positioning of barricades on approaches slowed the
advance of the British infantry down and funnelled them into

kill zones overlooked by strong points. A number of these strong points, such as 'Reilly's Fort' [21] and 'Langan's Public House' [7], were supported by fire from other positions. This created interlocking arcs of fire which meant that every inch of ground was covered. Rifle fire criss-crossed the area and kept all movement to a minimum, slowing the advance of British forces into the city. House-to-house fighting also contributed to draining British resources, and necessitated a huge expenditure of ammunition and manpower. Daly's positioning of his men obtained maximum effect and mutual supporting fire enabling long-range engagements. Many of the Volunteers were excellent shots, and Daly's use of sniper fire inflicted numerous casualties on the enemy and undermined their morale. Daly showed excellent military skills by adapting his plans to suit his small mobilisation strength. He kept up constant communication with Volunteer Headquarters at the General Post Office until his Battalion were cut off on Thursday of Easter week.

However, Daly's failure to occupy Broadstone Railway Station [12] and the destruction of Linenhall barracks [6] greatly weakened his position in the area. The British Army quickly occupied the station, giving them a vantage point that enabled them to keep up a continuous fire into the Volunteer positions. Though the deliberate setting fire to Linenhall Barracks improved morale among the Volunteers, it greatly assisted the British by tying down men in trying to control the fire. The occupation of the Mendicity Institute [2] on the South Quays was intended to block any advance by British forces on the Four Courts as the Volunteers established their positions early on Monday morning. This small post tied up large numbers of British troops and harassed any movement of troops along the quays. Considering the post was only to be occupied for a few hours, the garrison managed to hold the position, harass enemy forces and inflict numerous casualties for three days. This position also delayed the British advance on Sackville Street by a number of days. On the ground, outstanding leadership and initiative at every level of command maximised the Irish Volunteers' opportunities, and the British were repeatedly surprised by entrenched Volunteer positions in the area.

The British High Command reacted swiftly to the 1916 Rising. Military forces were entering the city by noon on the first day of the rebellion, and reinforcements from England were in position by Wednesday. The plan to retake the city by General Lowe was sound, and this was confirmed by General Sir John Grenfell Maxwell, who supported Lowe's Plans. In relation to the battle in and around the Four Courts area, General Sir John Grenfell Maxwell stated:

Our policy during the suppression of the rebellion was to put a military cordon around the chief rebel area in Sackville Street, but when we had done so we discovered that there was another centre of importance at the Four Courts, and we determined also to encircle that. One line of this cordon was to pass through North King Street. We discovered, however, that instead of being outside the rebel area, this line actually cut through it, and very desperate fighting occurred before we could complete the cordon in this street. With the one exception of the place at Ballsbridge, where the Sherwood Foresters were ambushed, this was by far the worst fighting that occurred in the whole of Dublin. At first the troops, coming from the end of one street, were repulsed, and it was only when we made an attack from both ends that we succeeded after twenty-four hours' fighting in capturing the street.[4]

Urban warfare is very different than fighting in the country-side, where each platoon or company can support one another. In the close confines of a city, the battlefield is fragmented and each unit must fight in isolation, supported only by the assets attached to it.

On the ground, the military tactics employed by Lieutenant-Colonel Taylor of the South Staffordshire regiment were very advanced for the time. Having realised that he was attacking well-prepared defensive positions, Taylor used his initiative in order to deploy his men and carry out his orders. The use of improvised armoured personnel vehicles to ferry troops to forward positions supported by machine-gun fire contributed greatly to keeping British casualties to a minimum. The landscape of a battlefield has often been used to conceal movement and to protect an army from fire. Taylor used the method of tunnelling from house to house in order to advance and keep British casualties low. The British Army also used the tactic of 'marching fire'. This meant firing constantly at likely hiding places as you advanced, rather than waiting for an identifiable target. After the initial attacks, the British commander realised that in order to seal the cordon on North King Street he would have to launch simultaneous attacks from east and west. It was only through this change of tactics that the British managed to seal the cordon on the street. The young British recruits disliked house-to-house fighting. They found such close-quarter combat, which broke conventional military boundaries and dimensions, psychologically disorientating. Urban combat proved stressful and chaotic for both sides during the Easter Rising. In a war zone every city, every road and every building is a potential death-trap. Nerves were fraught as British troops and Irish Volunteers fought from house to house, clearing rooms and fighting at point-blank range.

The ferocity of the fighting in Dublin can never be in doubt. There were 60,000 square yards of buildings destroyed, with an estimated cost of £2.4 million sterling.

Combat losses are difficult to fully ascertain during and after the 1916 Rising. It is estimated that British forces suffered 550 casualties killed or wounded, the Irish Volunteers about 215 killed or wounded. While many groups, both military and civilian, kept records of the deaths during Easter week, many fail to include people who died of combat wounds years after they were inflicted.

One factor that must not be overlooked in fighting in a built-up area is the humanitarian one. During the fighting of Easter week 1916, there were more civilian casualties than military or Volunteers. It is estimated that 2,500 civilians were killed or wounded during Easter week. The casualty rates for the 1916 Irish Rising may be far higher than those recorded. Civilian casualty figures for many wars are almost impossible to verify, as fighting in a built up area such as a town or city can result in a large number of civilian deaths. Even when civilians are evacuated from the combat area, many choose to ignore the instruction to move or return before the fighting has finished. In Dublin city, many civilians were shot dead for disobeying orders issued by the Irish Volunteers, or were killed by British military personnel who suspected them of being part of the enemy. The Rising also awakened atavistic instincts, and transformed a number of citizens into looters. Some were shot for this crime, but the majority of civilian deaths were those caught in the cross-fire between British troops and Irish Volunteers.

Historically, civilians have constituted half of all war deaths, largely the result of being targeted intentionally by belligerents in campaigns that include massacre, bombardments, starvation and destruction of the means of life.[5]

When commanding officers and men become isolated from the realities of the battlefield, they lose sight of the morality of what they are trying to achieve. In fighting in a built-up area, the line between legitimate and illegitimate killing often becomes blurred. On a battlefield, where does the responsibility lie?

> Military commanders may also be responsible for war crimes committed by their subordinates. When troops commit massacres and atrocities against the civilian population of occupied territory or against prisoners of war, the responsibility may rest not only with the actual perpetrators but also with the commander. Such a responsibility arises directly when the acts in question have been committed in pursuance of an order of the commander concerned. The commander is also responsible if he has actual knowledge, or should have knowledge, through reports received by him or through other means, that troops or persons subject to his control are about to commit or have committed a war crime and he fails to take the necessary and reasonable steps to insure compliance with the law of war or to punish violators thereof.[6]

Today, throughout the world, wars are being fought in cities, towns and villages. Soldiers are continuously facing civilians in armed conflicts. The policy of free-fire zones, in which a soldier is permitted to shoot at any human target, armed or unarmed, further contributes to the confusion of a soldier's moral senses.

At the beginning of the twentieth century, only 10-15% of those who died in war were civilians. As World War Two came to end, 50% of those who died were civilians. By the end of the twentieth century, over 75% of those killed in war were civilians.[7]

'Collateral damage' has become the buzz-word for civilian deaths, a sad factor of today's world – a world that accepts the death of innocents.

Today, throughout the world, soldiers are still seeing red.

Epilogue

Echoes of our past have been slowly eroded, and now all that remains are memories. We have been aware for some time that the anniversaries in relation to the 1916 Rising serve to remind us that this historic event is passing into the realms of history, and there is no one left from either side to give a first-hand account of events. While many choose to forget our turbulent past, others choose to reminisce selectively. Forgotten are the deaths and destruction visited on Dublin city during Easter week 1916. The Rising of 1916, the Irish War of Independence and the Civil War are considered to be essential steps towards Irish independence, yet each saw a considerable level of death and destruction.

It is sometimes said that if you haven't been in war, you have no business passing judgment on the warriors. Few people have any experience of real war. Regular soldiers can serve their careers without ever experiencing first hand the horror of battle. It is after the battle, when the field is strewn with the dead and wounded, that the full horror of war makes itself felt. At a general level one does not hear the guns, see the dead, feel the fear or know any combat. Winston Groom, the author of *Forrest Gump*, writes 'that trying to describe one's military experiences

111

is like trying to describe the colour blue to a blind man. You try to remember that you must not cross over from war into murder. In the brutality of combat, life is cheap. Then you come back to the civilian world, where life is precious. It's surreal.'[1]

Many questions, political, military and ethical, still arise in relation to the insurrection. When confronted with the facts of this event it is difficult to be impartial. The legacy of the 1916 Rising is that it still provokes debate, discussion and disagreement among the population, as it rightfully should.

Endnotes

Chapter 1
1 O' Duffy, S., Witness Statement W/S 313 (Bureau of Military History 1913-1921, Dublin)
2 Dowling, T.,Witness Statement W/S 533 (Bureau of Military History 1913-1921, Dublin)
3 Dublin Metropolitan Police
4 Stephenson, Patrick, *Heuston's Fort* (Whitegate, Co. Cork, 1966)
5 Stephenson, Patrick, *Heuston's Fort* (Whitegate, Co. Cork, 1966)

Chapter 2
1 Holohan, G., Witness Statement W/S 328 (Bureau of Military History 1913-1921, Dublin)

Chapter 3
1 Statement 75/92/1 A.C. Hannant, Imperial War Museum

Chapter 4
1 Holohan, P., *The Capuchin Annual* (Dollard, Dublin, 1966) p. 184
2 O' Carroll, L., Witness Statement W/S 314 (Bureau of Military History 1913-1921, Dublin)

3 Bradbridge, E.U., *59th Division 1915-1918* (Wilfred Edmunds, Chesterfield, 1928)

Chapter 5
1 *The War History of The 2/6th South Staffordshire* (William Heinemann Ltd., London, 1924)
2 O' Carroll, L. Witness Statement W/S 314 (Bureau of Military History 1913-1921, Dublin)
3 Caulfield, Max, *The Easter Rebellion* (Gill & Macmillan, Dublin, 1995)
4 Holohan, G., Witness Statement W/S 328 (Bureau of Military History 1913-1921, Dublin)

Chapter 7
1 *The War History of The 2/6th South Staffordshire* (William Heinemann Ltd., London, 1924)
2 O' Brien, P., *Blood on the Streets, 1916 & The Battle for Mount Street Bridge* (Mercier Press, Cork, 2008)
3 O' Carroll, L., Witness Statement W/S 314 (Bureau of Military History 1913-1921, Dublin)
4 Kelly, P., Witness Statement W/S 78 (Bureau of Military History 1913-1921, Dublin)
5 Reynolds, J., *An t-Óglác*, May 1926

Chapter 8
1 O' Dea, M., Witness Statement W/S 115.2 (Bureau of Military History 1913-1921, Dublin)
2 Rooney, C., Witness Statement W/S 648 (Bureau of Military History 1913-1921, Dublin)

Chapter 9
1 *The War History of The 2/6th South Staffordshire* (William

Heinemann Ltd., London, 1924)
2 01/59/1 W/S Henry James Davis, Imperial War Museum
3 O' Duffy, S., Witness Statement W/S 313 (Bureau of
Military History 1913-1921, Dublin)
4 Oates, W.C., *The 2/8th Battalion, The Sherwood Foresters in the
Great War* (J&H Bell Ltd., Nottingham, 1921)
5 McHugh, Roger, *Dublin 1916* (Arlington Books, London, 1976)
6 Caulfield, Max, *The Easter Rebellion* (Gill & Macmillan,
Dublin, 1995)
7 Kelly, P., Witness Statement W/S 781 (Bureau of Military
History 1913-1921, Dublin)
8 Maxwell, Sir J.G., Public Proclamation issued 28th April
1916

Chapter 10
1 Caulfield, Max, *The Easter Rebellion* (Gill & Macmillan,
Dublin, 1995)
2 Flanagan, M., Witness Statement W/S 800 (Bureau of
Military History 1913-1921, Dublin)
3 Flanagan, M., Witness Statement W/S 800 (Bureau of
Military History 1913-1921, Dublin)

Chapter 11
1 Reynolds, J., *An t-Óglác*, May 1926
2 O' Connell, M., Witness Statement W/S 804 (Bureau of
Military History 1913-1921, Dublin)
3 Reynolds, J., *An t-Óglác*, May 1926
4 Holohan, G., Witness Statement W/S 328 (Bureau of
Military History 1913-1921, Dublin)
5 Kelly, P., Witness Statement W/S 781 (Bureau of Military
History 1913-1921, Dublin)

6 Holohan, P., *The Capuchin Annual* (Dollard, Dublin, 1966)

Chapter 12

1 McHugh, Roger, *Dublin 1916* (Arlington Books, London, 1976)
2 Caulfield, Max, *The Easter Rebellion* (Gill & Macmillan, Dublin, 1995)
3 Béaslaí, P., *Dublin's Fighting Story* (Mercier Press, Cork, 2009)
4 Holohan, G., Witness Statement W/S 328 (Bureau of Military History 1913-1921, Dublin)

Chapter 13

1 Reynolds, J., *An t-Óglác*, May 1926
2 Ui Chonail, É., *The Capuchin Annual* (Dollard, Dublin, 1966) p. 184
3 Morkan, E., Witness Statement W/S 411 (Bureau of Military History 1913-1921, Dublin)

Chapter 14

1 PRO WO 71/348
2 Mac Lochlainn, P.F., *Last Words* (Dúchas, Dublin, 1990)
3 Mac Lochlainn, P.F., *Last Words* (Dúchas, Dublin, 1990) p. 74
4 PRO WO71/348
5 Mac Lochlainn, P.F., *Last Words* (Dúchas, Dublin, 1990) p. 116
6 Hall, W.G., *The Green Triangle* (Naval & Military Press, Uckfield, East Sussex, 2009)
7 Maxwell to Asquith, 10 May 1916, Asquith Papers, MS43, Bodleian Library, Oxford University

Chapter 15

1 WO 141/21
2 WO 141/21

3 WO 141/21
4 Taylor, Lieutenant-Colonel H., *The Irish Times*, May 1916
5 Maxwell, Sir J.G, *Daily Mail*, May 1916

Chapter 16
1 Maxwell, Sir J.G, Headquarters, Irish Command, 1 May 1916
2 O' Dea, M., Witness Statement W/S 115.2 (Bureau of Military History 1913-1921, Dublin)
3 Breen, D., *My Fight For Irish Freedom* (Anvil Books, Dublin, 1978)

Chapter 17
1 Von Clausewitz, Carl, *On War* (ed. & trans. Michael Howard & Peter Paret, Princeton University Press, Princeton, 1832/1976)
2 Hally, Colonel P.J., 'The Easter 1916 Rising in Dublin: The Military Aspects', *The Irish Sword* (Dublin, 1966)
3 *The War History of The 2/6th South Staffordshire* (William Heinemann Ltd., London, 1924)
4 Maxwell, Sir J.G., *Daily Mail,* Thursday 18 May 1916
5 Eckhardt, W., *Civilian Deaths in Wartime*, Bulletin of Peace Proposals, 1989
6 Prosecution Brief on the Law of Principals in United States v. Captain Ernest L. Medina
7 Hills, A.E., *Future War in Cities: Rethinking a Liberal Dilemma* (Frank Cass, London, 2004)

Epilogue
1. *Time* magazine, 2001

Select Bibliography

Béaslaí, P., *Dublin's Fighting Story* (Mercier Press, Cork, 2009)

Bradbridge, E.U., *59th Division 1915-1918* (Wilfred Edmunds, Chesterfield, 1928)

Caulfield, M., *The Easter Rebellion* (Gill & Macmillan, Dublin, 1995)

Hall, W.G., *The Green Triangle* (Naval & Military Press, Uckfield, East Sussex, 2009)

McHugh, R., *Dublin 1916* (Arlington Books, London, 1976)

Mac Lochlainn, P.F., *Last Words* (Dúchas, Dublin, 1990)

O' Brien, P., *Blood on the Streets, 1916 & The Battle for Mount Street Bridge* (Mercier Press, Cork, 2008)

Oates, W.C., *The 2/8th Battalion, The Sherwood Foresters in the Great War* (J&H Bell Ltd., Nottingham, 1921)

Rees, R., *Ireland 1905-25: Vol 1. Text and Historiography* (Colour Print Books, Newtownards, 1998)

Stephenson, Patrick, *Heuston's Fort* (Whitegate, Co. Cork, 1966)

The War History of The 2/6th South Staffordshire (William Heinemann Ltd., London, 1924)

Von Clausewitz, Carl, *On War* (ed. & trans. Michael Howard & Peter Paret, Princeton University Press, Princeton, 1832/1976)

Index

Coming Soon in the

1916 IN FOCUS

Series...

Field of Fire: 1916 & The Battle of Ashbourne

Paul O'Brien

While Dublin city has acquired a certain romanticism in fictional and factual accounts of the 1916 Rising, real dramas were also taking place outside the capital city. North County Dublin and County Meath, with their lush vegetation and green fields, were home to much Volunteer activity in April 1916.

The town of Ashbourne, historically known as Cill Dhéagláin, is located twenty kilometres north of Dublin city. It was at Ashbourne in County Meath on Friday 28 April 1916 that the Royal Irish Constabulary found themselves in action against the forces of the 5th Battalion of the Irish Volunteers.

In many of the works written on the 1916 Easter Rising, the Battle of Ashbourne has been ignored, and dismissed as a side show to what was taking place in Dublin city. On studying the engagement, however, it can be seen that it was not only an integral part of the Rising, but also a template for future tactics and strategies employed by Republican forces during the Irish War of Independence.

The Battle of Ashbourne was a complicated and bloody affair, and poses a number of questions for the student of military history. Questions arise in relation to the strategy employed by the police, and the controversy that surrounded the number of casualties they suffered and whether they could have been avoided. Was the action that took place an ambush, as it was characterised by the Crown, or was there much more to the battle?

With regard to the Irish side, questions emerge concerning the military competence of their force during the battle and how they managed to pull off one of the greatest victories of the 1916 Rising.

Unlike castles and cathedrals, the rural battlefields of the 1916 Rising are not easily found, and require some background knowledge of the contenders' tactics, the cause of the battle and the reasons for its final outcome. At first sight, Ashbourne is a piece of rural landscape. Yet it was here that forces of the Royal Irish Constabulary were defeated in a bloody conflict. The object of this book is to describe the battle that took place and dispel many of the myths that have grown up around this significant historical engagement.

ISBN 978-1-84840-156-3
Publishing autumn 2012

126